"Trevin Wax faithfully sounds the call for world-changing, Christ-exalting Christian practice. By unmasking contemporary 'Caesars,' he reveals real dangers and points to pitfalls of which many believers are completely unaware. This book serves as a helpful reminder and competent guide to draw out the implications of true allegiance to Jesus Christ."

Al Mohler, President, The Southern Baptist Theological Seminary

"How should God's American people put the lordship of Jesus Christ on display in their lives? Wax's searching answer is biblical, basic, businesslike, and blunt."

J. I. Packer, Professor of Theology, Regent College

"Trevin Wax passionately tackles some of the most dangerous idols in our culture, and, unfortunately, in our own lives. Especially relevant now is his reminder to us of the way money can capture us and force us into submission. Not only in days of economic stress, but also in those of economic prosperity, we must be aware of money's alluring trap and learn how to turn this resource into something that may be used for the kingdom. With judicious insights and clear writing on a number of issues, Wax challenges us to live subversively against the powers of this world."

Johnny M. Hunt, Pastor, First Baptist Church of Woodstock, GA; President, The Southern Baptist Convention

"Christianity is all about paradox. We lose our lives to gain them. We find life in crucifixion. We serve in order to reign. In his book, *Holy Subversion*, Trevin Wax takes up the question of how to be both a rebel—against the false authorities of this time—while simultaneously being submissive—to the divine authority of the God and Father of our Lord Jesus Christ. This book is a helpful warning against both nihilism and cynicism."

Russell D. Moore, Dean, The Southern Baptist Theological Seminary; author, *The Kingdom of Christ* and *Adopted for Life*

"Simple yet succinct, *Holy Subversion* exposes the idols of modernity and provides the biblical arsenal needed for their complete destruction. Trevin Wax provides medicine for the heart in this short, powerful study. Read it and be blessed."

Daniel L. Akin, President, Southeastern Baptist Theological Seminary

"Trevin Wax provides good advice on how to turn away from the idols of success, money, leisure, sex. and power."

Marvin Olasky, Provost, The King's College; Editor-in-Chief, *World*

"Using a definition of subversion as 'pushing something back down into its proper place,' Trevin Wax seeks to subvert the idols of our society—self, success, money, leisure, sex, and power—in a theologically responsible and challengingly practical way. These false gods must be thrust back into their proper place, and that subversion is precisely what the gospel of Jesus Christ—the message about the crucified and resurrected God-man who is Lord over all bogus lords—equips us to do. Wax wonders, 'What would it look like today if we reclaimed the subversive nature of Christian discipleship?' Read this fine book if you wish to live as the true Savior and Lord Jesus Christ would have you live."

Gregg R. Allison, Professor of Christian Theology,
The Southern Baptist Theological Seminary

"The Apostle John warns us to 'keep ourselves from idols.' Trevin Wax, in this incisive, convicting, and elegantly written book, considers the false gods that insidiously corrupt our lives. I was reminded afresh what it means to confess that Jesus is Lord and that glorifying God expresses itself in the concrete realities of daily life. What a joy to read a book that is theologically faithful and practically compelling."

Thomas R. Schreiner, James Buchanan Harrison Professor of
New Testament Interpretation, The Southern Baptist Theological Seminary

"In *Holy Subversion*, Trevin Wax issues a wide-ranging invitation for believers to rethink what it means to be a Christ-follower in a culture that offers rival ways of thinking and living at every turn. Those who wrestle with this timely and biblically-based challenge will be called to nothing less than whole-hearted faithfulness in all areas of life."

David Dockery, President, Union University

"In the midst of much debate and uncertainly about the kingdom of God in the world today, Wax makes it clear that Jesus' kingdom challenges our allegiances. Wax looks at issues of idolatry and strongholds that, one by one, show us how the gospel of the kingdom requires a new loyalty. *Holy Subversion* is a helpful and challenging book."

Ed Stetzer, President, LifeWay Research; author, *Lost and Found*

"With Francis Schaeffer-like instincts and insight, Trevin Wax aptly identifies the idols of our time and compellingly calls Christians to live against the world, for the world. He blazes a trustworthy trail for those who yearn to make a long lasting difference in the world by showing that Christians make a difference by being different; they don't make a difference by being the same."

Tullian Tchividjian, Pastor, Coral Ridge Presbyterian Church;
author, *Unfashionable: Making a Difference in this World
by Being Different*

"There is the sense that something is wrong in the church, very wrong, and most prognosticators have been telling us what we need to do get back on track. Trevin Wax takes a different approach, a more radical approach—he calls us to come face to face with the 'Caesars' in our life. Only once we have understood the dire effect of these allegiances, as Wax shows, can we then hope to subvert the kingdoms vying for our localities. *Holy Subversion* makes clear the contours of the sacred revolution which is ours to undertake."

> **Nicholas Perrin**, Franklin S. Dyrness Chair of Biblical Studies
> Associate Professor of New Testament, Wheaton College; author,
> *Lost in Transmission? What We Can Know about the Words of Jesus*

"Today we live in a land of self-made men who love to worship the creators of their success. Sadly, this very same attitude has crept into the church. Quite rightly then, Trevin Wax challenges us to see what it means to confess Jesus Christ as Lord: to embrace and rejoice in the sovereignty of Jesus Christ over all things. But this book is not about the doctrine of Jesus' lordship; it is about how you live out Jesus' lordship in every sphere of your life. In an age where there are many 'gods' and many 'lords' bidding for our allegiance, Trevin Wax calls the church to throw down these idols and to order their lives according to the story, symbols, and values of the Lord Jesus Christ. He encourages us to get our knees dirty by bowing to Christ and our hands dirty by serving him. This is a book that every serious follower of Jesus should read and heed."

> **Michael F. Bird**, Highland Theological College/UHI Millennium Institute

"Trevin Wax deftly uses Scripture and his cross-cultural experience in Romania to convict North American Christians of the subtle ways that we conform to our culture's idols. His tough love inspires us to surrender to Jesus' ownership of the world, and his bold plan for change shows us how. This book forces each of us to reconsider the most important question of our lives: whether Caesar or Jesus is Lord."

> **Michael Wittmer**, Professor of Systematic Theology, Grand Rapids
> Theological Seminary; author, *Heaven Is a Place on Earth* and
> *Don't Stop Believing*

"In this book, Trevin Wax returns us to a God-centeredness displayed in the Scriptures. He reminds us that faithfulness is more important than success, humility more desirous than fame, and Christian unity can be achieved even in the face of great diversity. I highly recommend this for anyone seeking an authentic relationship with the God who transforms our lives, our passions, and our world."

> **Christian George**, author, *Sex, Sushi, and Salvation: Thoughts on Intimacy, Community, and Eternity*

"In *Holy Subversion*, Trevin Wax engages both the church and the world with clarity and conviction. With great insight into the heart of the apostolic gospel, Wax highlights the profound impact of early Christians' complete allegiance to Jesus of Nazareth as Savior and Lord over all aspects of personal life and society. True Christianity, contends the author, dethrones the Caesar of our day and enthrones Jesus Christ as the only Savior and Lord over all life. This is a timely and prophetic book for our generation. I highly recommend it to pastors, evangelists, missionaries, Sunday-school teachers, and all believers in Jesus Christ. Jesus Christ's life, death, and resurrection and the empowering presence of the Holy Spirit, according to the inspired and infallible Word of God, represents the foundation for the author's call to contemporary Christians to the 'Ephesians Road,' that is, to live and labor with undivided loyalty for the glory of one and the only Master of time and eternity, Jesus Christ."

Paul Negrut, President, Emanuel University of Oradea, Romania

"Trevin Wax delivers a sober challenge for the church to live up to her lofty calling. By God's grace, may Christians heed his warning and follow the narrow path prepared by Jesus. Perhaps we will then see the fruit of the Spirit's transforming power in our midst."

Collin Hansen, Editor-at-Large, *Christianity Today*;
author, *Young, Restless, Reformed: A Journalist's Journey with the New Calvinists*

"The bridge between the biblical world and ours is a two-way path. Most travelers start from the Here-and-Now world and, equipped with the tools of exegesis, step back in space-time into the There-and-Then world. Trevin Wax makes a bold proposal for a journey in the opposite direction. What would it be like if the biblical authors were to step into our own world? How would Moses, David, Paul, or even Jesus proclaim God's message if they were living today? The author's creative and persuasive proposal invites the readers to ponder what they might plausibly hear if the biblical imperative against idolatry were given to us today."

Radu Gheorghita, Professor of New Testament,
Midwestern Baptist Theological Seminary

"This book reads like a series of very good sermons. There is pastoral wisdom, balance, and conviction in these pages. Trevin Wax helps us remember what really matters."

Kevin DeYoung, author, *Why We're Not Emergent* and
Just Do Something

HOLY SUBVERSION

HOLY SUBVERSION

Allegiance to Christ in an Age of Rivals

TREVIN WAX

FOREWORD BY ED STETZER

CROSSWAY

WHEATON, ILLINOIS

Trade paperback ISBN: 978-1-4335-0702-1

PDF ISBN: 978-1-4335-0703-8

Mobipocket ISBN: 978-1-4335-0704-5

ePub ISBN: 978-1-4335-2341-0

Library of Congress Cataloging-in-Publication Data
Wax, Trevin, 1981–
   Holy subversion : allegiance to Christ in an age of rivals /
Trevin Wax ; foreword by Ed Stetzer.
     p. cm.
   Includes bibliographical references.
   ISBN 978-1-4335-0702-1 (tpb)
   1. Christian life. 2. Jesus Christ—Lordship. I. Title.
BV4509.5.W3745   2010
248—dc22   2009014506

VP		18	17	16	15	14	13	12	11	10
13	12	11	10	9	8	7	6	5	4	3	2	1

For
Corina
iubita mea

CONTENTS

FOREWORD

IN HIS "HIGH PRIESTLY PRAYER," Jesus, who knew his betrayal, arrest, torture, and crucifixion lay mere hours away, nevertheless prays for the community of his followers. For three years, this carpenter-king and his band of misfit disciples set about teaching and living the presence of the kingdom of heaven.

This kingdom didn't look like earthly kingdoms, and, in fact, in many ways it was the opposite of every kingdom first-century cultures were accustomed to. The truth, of course, is that those earthly kingdoms were corrupt versions of the real, eternal kingdom. For this reason among many others, both King Jesus and the kingdom of God were (and are) radically countercultural.

In those anguished moments of intercession, Jesus says to the Father, "My prayer is not that you take them out of the world but that you protect them from the evil one. They are not of the world, even as I am not of it." This is why the kingdom of God, where Jesus' followers are still called to live, is always countercultural—or, rather, why it *should* be.

The church was never meant to go along with the world; it was supposed to stand out. The church received the charge from Jesus himself to continue the witness of their King and his kingdom. The church was meant to be "in the world, but not of it." Ironically, in our earnest and sincere efforts to transform the culture around us, we have actually been transformed ourselves. Instead of being salt and light, we have become *unsalted* and *lite*.

A 2002 Barna Research study indicates "a large share of the people who attend Protestant or Catholic churches have adopted beliefs that conflict with the teachings of the Bible and their church." Another revealed that 54 percent of those identifying themselves as "born again Christians" believe that moral truth "depends on the situation."[1] Numerous surveys have confirmed that the unchurched may be interested in Jesus, but they think the church is full of hypocrites. Whether this perception is fair or not, it certainly is not the result of an overwhelming number of Christians living in accordance with their beliefs.

In a 2007–2008 study, LifeWay Research found disconcerting results when looking at the views and practices of 2,500 Protestant churchgoers. Among the more discouraging revelations is that only 50 percent indicated they choose God's way over their own way when faced with a difficult decision. Only 53 percent indicated they give 10 percent or more of their finances to charity, including their local church. Additional questions on anxiety, forgiveness, and correcting wrongdoings indicate the church may be more similar to the world than we'd like to think.

In his book *The Shape of Faith to Come*, Brad Waggoner presents even more sobering data.[2] Among his findings, Waggoner reports that only 16 percent of Protestant churchgoers read their Bible daily and another 20 percent read it only a few times a week. Just 23 percent "agreed strongly" with the statement, "When I come to realize that some aspect of my life is not right in God's eyes, I make the necessary changes." A full 47 percent of Protestant churchgoers admitted to often just "going through the motions" during the singing and prayer portions of worship services. The interesting thing is that the survey respondents actually believed they were experiencing significant spiritual growth. But according to the Spiritual Formation Inventory evaluation tool, only 3.5 percent of respondents showed a significant level of spiritual growth a year later.

The evangelical church must own up to the frustrating possibility that we are not as effective at making disciples as we think we are.

As the church rides the waves of a changing culture, struggling to do the *necessary* work of contextualizing its message and practice to diverse environments, it has become evident that many have overcompensated. Like Paul, we seek to become like all men in order to win some, but for many of us this has meant becoming indistinguishable from all men. It's not cultural contextualization we've achieved, but cultural capitulation.

Like Israel, the church has gone after the gods of the nations. The idols of self, success, money, leisure/entertainment, sex, and power are enduring lures, and unfortunately have even been employed by the church as lures in its fishing for men. It was idolatry the prophets rebuked Israel for; it was idolatry Jesus called his followers out of; and it is idolatry the church must call the nations out of. We must start by repenting ourselves and resuming the prophetic mantle of radical worship of the resurrected King.

In the movie *The League of Extraordinary Gentlemen*, seven unlikely characters form a subversive alliance to thwart The Phantom, a stealth enemy who plans to conquer the world by bringing about an Armageddon-like war. As the villain and his henchmen are capturing a German professor, the professor asks what the diabolical character wants. The Phantom replies, "The world, Herr Draper. I want the world!"

As the movie unfolds, the league learns to trust one another and work together in order to defeat their unknown enemy, especially after they figure out who the traitor in their group is. They are willing to risk resources and their very own lives to stop their evil enemy and save the world from destruction. In the same way, God has called the church of Jesus Christ to join him on a mission to save the people of the world from sin (the internal enemy), Satan (our stealth enemy), and eternal death (the end for those without Christ).

When Jesus started his earthly ministry, he formed a subversive alliance with twelve other men. Their enemies were sin and Satan. With his motley crew, Jesus spoke about faith, followership, love, kingdom, and righteousness, all beginning with allegiance to his lordship, which of course begins with repentance from all other lordships.

Trevin Wax calls this life of repentance "holy subversion," and in this book you will hear loud and clear how allegiance to Christ mandates it. If Jesus is King of kings and Lord of lords, then Caesar is not.

Chapter by chapter, Wax invites us to cast down the "Caesars" of our own making and lay down our crowns before the throne of God, and he shows us—biblically and practically— how to do it. To be a kingdom people, after all, we must raze our idols and raise our crosses.

Consider some of the things Jesus said about his lordship:

- "You shall worship the Lord your God and him only shall you serve" (Matt. 4:10).
- "Not everyone who says to me, 'Lord, Lord,' will enter the kingdom of heaven, but the one who does the will of my Father who is in heaven" (Matt. 7:21).
- "Love the Lord your God with all your heart and with all your soul and with all your mind and with all your strength" (Mark 12:30).
- "Prepare the way of the Lord, make his paths straight" (Luke 3:4).
- "You shall not put the Lord your God to the test" (Luke 4:12).
- "Why do you call me, 'Lord, Lord,' and not do what I tell you?" (Luke 6:46).
- "Make straight the way of the Lord" (John 1:23).
- "If I then, your Lord and Teacher, have washed your feet, you also ought to wash one another's feet" (John 13:14).

It sounds like Jesus was pretty serious about this lordship stuff. Jesus' status as Lord is supposed to mean something to his followers; it should make a difference in the lives of his followers and, through them, spread to the world. That basic truth is really what Trevin has described in a masterful, practical, and relevant way in *Holy Subversion*. The lordship of Jesus Christ should permeate every area and aspect of the believer's life; that alliance with King Jesus should subvert the idolatrous forces of the heart and the culture to impact people all over the world with the gospel.

Those like me who have been fortunate enough to encounter Trevin's writing in print and online know his voice is a precious and rare one in a world of Christian "noise." With painstaking clarity and steadfast focus, Trevin never strays from the "first importance" of the gospel. Trevin is one of my favorite writers, but Trevin's writing is not, as it is for so many others, mere theoretical styling. From his service in the mission field of Romania to his pastoral ministry in the mission field of the Bible Belt, Trevin writes from a hard-won experience and a firsthand passion. His outright affection for the kingdom and its King has been cultivated by a Godward allegiance that has taken him to "the ends of the earth."

I know you will find Trevin's devoted affection for the things of God challenging, but I trust you will find his call to holy subversion stirring. To echo the description of the growing church in Acts 9:31, may the words that follow strengthen and encourage you to walk "in the fear of the Lord."

Ed Stetzer
www.edstetzer.com

1

JESUS AND THE GOSPEL OF CAESAR

LORD.
>Savior of the world.
>Son of God.
>Divine ruler.
>The news of his birth and his rule was called "the gospel."
>His fame was spread throughout the known world by special messengers.

The preachers of his gospel believed he had brought a reign of peace to the whole world, and that he had all authority in heaven and on earth.

Who is this man? If you were to visit a church and ask people to whom these titles and sayings refer, almost everyone would say "Jesus Christ." And rightly so. The Bible claims that Jesus is Lord, the Savior of the world, God's Son.

But let's say you were living in the first century under the rule of the Roman Empire. If you were to enter a town or city and ask people to whom these titles and slogans refer, they would answer differently. *Lord? Savior of the world? Son of God?* "Of course you must be talking about Caesar," they would say. In the first century, each of these titles described the Roman emperors—powerful men who ruled the world with an iron fist, demanding submission to the ever-expanding empire.[1]

The early Christians used some of the same titles given to

Caesar in their preaching about Jesus of Nazareth. Why did they do this? And what does this mean for us as Christians today?

THE WORLD TWO-THOUSAND YEARS AGO

Two-thousand years ago, at the helm of the burgeoning Roman Empire stood the Caesars, named after Julius Caesar, who lived during the first century BC. The early Caesars had been declared "divine" shortly after their deaths. Before long, the Caesars had begun accepting that title of worship during their lives. The emperors commissioned messengers to travel from town to town, preaching allegiance to Caesar. By the time of Jesus, the cult of Caesar worship had begun to spread throughout the empire.

First-century "heralds" visited the cities and villages of the Roman Empire, sharing the "gospel" (good news) of a Caesar's accession to the throne. As Caesar worship spread, those under Rome's authority were forced to bow down, confess Caesar as Lord, and pay the appropriate taxes. It didn't matter whether they approved of Caesar or not. Caesar was sovereign. He was the ruler. You refused to worship him at your own peril! Domitian, one of the late first-century Caesars went so far as to sign his documents, "God."[2]

At times, Rome could be surprisingly tolerant of other religions. A pantheon of deities was allowed in the Roman Empire as long as Caesar worship trumped them all. The highest loyalty was reserved for the earthly Caesar and his authority. All other rivals had to kneel before his throne. Jewish believers who believed in the one true God were a perfect target for Roman rulers and prefects, men like Pontius Pilate, who often intimidated their Jewish subjects by acts of senseless violence.[3]

THE FIRST CHRISTIANS

Into this highly charged atmosphere of oppression, a group of men and women began spreading a message about a crucified and risen Messiah. It was a message that would cost many their lives. The apostles ("sent-ones") took to the streets of Rome's cities as heralds, messengers of a new gospel. However, the good news they were sharing was about a Jewish Messiah's lordship over all creation, not a Caesar's accession to the throne. They began preaching that Jesus of Nazareth is the Son of God, the Lord of heaven and earth, and the Lord over Caesar himself. Their creed? "Jesus is Lord . . . and God raised him from the dead."[1]

Christians even took the honorific titles and sayings reserved for God in the Old Testament and applied them to Jesus himself. *There is no other name in heaven or on earth by which people can be saved.[5] All authority has been given to him.[6] At the name of Jesus, every knee will bow.[7]*

But these titles, derived from Jewish teaching about God, also confronted the Caesar-worship of the first century. The disciples made it clear that the Savior of the world was not the Caesar who provided peace for the nation and pacified people with bread. The Savior is Jesus, who restores us to God and neighbor, and who offers his own body as the bread of eternal life. The disciples recognized that Jesus was the true Lord of the world. Caesar was a phony, a caricature, a parody of the true God.[8]

And the message spread. Christianity began to expand beyond its Jewish heritage. Churches (communities made up of these followers of another king) began to rise up in dark corners of the Roman Empire.

As Rome increased her borders by capturing and enslaving nations and people groups, Christianity grew by proclaiming freedom from the slavery of sin and death.

As the Caesars offered bread to the hungry in order to stay in power, the Christians upstaged the rulers by feeding the hungry themselves in the name of Jesus, the true Lord of the world.

As Rome's livelihood depended on a wide gap between impoverished slaves and wealthy citizens, the early Christians subverted Rome's economic system by voluntarily selling their belongings, giving to the needy, and treating slaves as brothers and sisters in Christ.

The early Christians submitted nobly to Roman authority, understanding that Caesar did have lawful authority delegated to him by God. Ironically, even though the early Christians faced periods of intense persecution, they still believed that the government was a gift from God and that a king could have a legitimate right to the throne.[9] The Christians subverted the power of Caesar, not by secretly plotting a revolution, but by refusing to give Caesar the honor that belonged to Jesus himself! They believed Caesar needed to be "put in his place"—under the lordship of Jesus Christ. Whenever Caesar exploited his position of power by seeking to rule the world as "god," the Christians went about their lives, subverting his rule by pledging allegiance to his superior, the Jesus before whom even Caesar would one day bend the knee.

Why did the early Christians act this way? How could they advocate submission to Roman authority even as they subverted Roman exploitation? The answer lies in their understanding of the "powers and principalities" that stood *behind* the earthly, visible Caesar.[10] The early Christians knew that the earthly ruler was not the ultimate enemy. The Caesar-worship of their day pointed beyond the rule of mere men to the presence of the Evil One who seeks to keep people in bondage to sin and death.

THE "POWERS AND PRINCIPALITIES" TODAY

In the West, we no longer live under the tight-fisted reign of the Caesars of Rome. In modern-day democracy, we choose our leaders. We elect our representatives. We are our own "Caesar."

But even if our society is not run by a dictator and even if we are not forced to bow down and worship Caesar as Lord, the same "powers and principalities" that stood behind the Caesar-worship of first-century Rome continue to manifest their presence by dominating the lives of people all around us.

Western societies are not run by human Caesars occupying the throne of a nation's capital; however, our world still remains under the influence of Satan—the Evil One who seeks to hold people in his clutches by perverting God's gifts (success, money, leisure, sex, power) and propping them up until they take over our sin-infested hearts and occupy the throne that should belong to Jesus. Unfortunately, many of these "Caesars" go unchallenged by the Christian community. We need to embrace the subversive nature of the first-century message. We must also recognize the insidious nature of the "powers and principalities" from which we need deliverance.

Early Christians posed a threat to Caesar because their message centered on what happened to Jesus of Nazareth on the Sunday morning after his crucifixion. Caesar was not threatened by Christian missionaries telling people they needed a personal Savior, one who will come "to live in their hearts." He was threatened by a subversive community who believed that a Jewish Messiah had been physically raised from the dead, and who was then living according to the new reality that his resurrection had inaugurated.

The early Christians were persecuted and killed, not only because they had personal relationships with Jesus Christ, but also because they were proclaiming Jesus as Lord. They were applying Caesar's titles of honor to Jesus Christ. They were subverting the authority of Caesar by appealing to the lordship of Jesus.

LIFE-CHANGING AND WORLD-CHANGING FAITH

The lived-out faith of the early Christians was life changing. Just look at Peter, "the Rock," who—just weeks after denying he knew Jesus—proclaimed that "God has made him both Lord and Christ, this Jesus whom you crucified."[11] Or look at the apostle Paul: once a persecutor of Christians, he became Christianity's most ardent defender and most famous missionary. Or consider Jesus' own brother James, who once believed his brother to be a madman, only to later realize after Jesus' resurrection that Jesus was indeed Lord and Savior of the world.

Christianity changes lives. When people trust Jesus as Savior and confess him as Lord, they are transformed. Evangelicals, perhaps more than any other segment of Christianity, believe in the power of Christ to change lives.

But true Christianity is not merely *life*-changing. It is *world*-changing. In the first century, belief in Jesus as Lord ran counter to the claims of Caesar. The lifestyles of the early Christians were deeply subversive of the "powers and principalities" ruling the world. Though they certainly would have agreed that Jesus was their "personal" Lord and Savior, the essence of their gospel proclamation centered on Jesus as the Lord of all—not just Lord of their hearts, but of the whole world. The gospel message was less about people inviting Jesus into their hearts and more about people being invited into the kingdom community that represents God's heart for the world.

What is God's future for this world? The early Christians believed that God would one day bring restoration to this broken world. The universe would be redeemed. The faithful who had died would be raised and given glorified bodies. But most importantly, the early Christians believed that this future had *already* broken into the present. The work of restoration and redemption had begun. Through the work of Jesus Christ (his death and resurrection), the age-to-come had already arrived in this present world.

Even though it seemed the world was ruled by God-hating dictators, Christians clung to an unshakable faith that Jesus was already, in fact, ruling and that the day would come when their faith would be sight. The whole world would see Christ, the world's true King. With boldness and confidence, the early Christians understood the need to begin living in the present according to the future reality, and so they sought to live under the reign of their King.

What would it look like today if we reclaimed the subversive nature of Christian discipleship? How would the royal announcement that Jesus is Lord change our mind-sets with regard to our churches, our families, our jobs? How can our allegiance to Jesus as King be *subversive* once again?

SUBVERTING THE CAESARS OF TODAY

When I was eight years old, my parents took me to a local high school football game. I didn't understand much about how the game was played, so my favorite part of the experience was watching the marching band perform a rousing rendition of Tchaikovsky's *1812 Overture* during half-time. The inspiring melody passionately performed by the band created an electrically charged atmosphere in that stadium that overwhelmed my childhood senses. I left the stadium believing I had just heard the most beautiful music ever composed.

A couple weeks later, we went to another football game. This time, I decided to take a battery-operated tape recorder with me. I waited anxiously for half-time, and when the band began playing, I pressed "record" on the tape player. I sat back and smiled, convinced that the awe-inspiring music filling the stadium would soon fill my room at home whenever I so desired.

That evening, I discovered that the playback quality on my tape player was less than stellar. The drums made popping sounds on the tape. The flutes and trumpets sounded like something from a horror movie. My spirit deflated. How was it that the music that had been so glorious in the stadium sounded so terrible in my room? I asked my dad why the tape couldn't recreate that beautiful music from the stadium. Dad replied, "Some music isn't meant for your room."

The gospel isn't meant for just me in my room. The beautiful music that comes from God's people gathered in worship and united in service isn't meant to be performed by one person in one place. The declaration that Jesus is Lord sounds most glorious when it is proclaimed through his church.

When we tailor the gospel only for individuals and make the message solely about a private religious experience, we wind up with a "cassette-tape gospel" that captures a sliver of the message but cannot do justice to the glorious melody of Christ's lordship playing all throughout creation. It is true that the church is made up of individuals who believe that Jesus is Lord. But *together* we form the called-out community of faith: the church—an orchestra divinely commissioned to play the music that proclaims salvation in Jesus Christ alone.

So, how can we *as communities of faith* live in a way that subverts the "Caesars" that rule people around us . . . and seek to rule us too? The rest of this book is devoted to answering that question.

There are two ways to understand the word "subvert" or "subversion." The first definition refers to "overthrowing" or plotting the downfall of a kingdom. The second way that "subverting" something is commonly understood refers to "undermining" or "pushing something back down into its proper place." In this book, I use the term "subversive" in the second sense. Each of the "Caesars" that we will deal with in this book are good gifts from God that become idolatrous when they are placed above God himself. Therefore, our job as Christians is first to identify and unmask some of the more insidious "Caesars" that seek to muzzle our message and demand our allegiance. Then, we must think through specific ways in which the church can counter our culture by subverting its prevailing idolatries and pushing them back to their rightful place, under the feet of Jesus.

The Caesar of Self

The first Caesar is the Caesar of Self. Consider the prominence of self-help books, narcissistic fads and diets, and the failed self-esteem movement. Western society is clearly in a love affair with the self, replete with phrases such as "You deserve it," and "Treat yourself." We have bought into the rampant individual-ism of our culture; this explains why thousands of professing Christians can claim Christianity as their personal religion and even believe they possess a superior spiritual life, while never set-ting foot in a local church or submitting to an outside spiritual authority.

As a community of believers, we subvert the self whenever we preach the gospel that comes to us from outside. Salvation has been accomplished *for* us, by someone else. The cross-centered life is one of continual dying to self and living for God.

The part of the gospel message that we evangelicals tend to leave out is precisely the part that strikes at the heart of the Caesar of Self: the gospel is intended to create a kingdom com-munity—and this community by corporate witness and action declares (in a way that individuals by themselves cannot) that Jesus is Lord.

The gospel unites us to the body of Christ, wherein we find

our true identity as children of God. Communities of faith are subversive when they place their own personal happiness aside and find joy in putting others first.

The Caesar of Success

We will also look at ways in which we can subvert the Caesar of Success. Western culture equates success with affluence. Wealth and influence bring power and prestige. We live in a culture that prizes success above everything else. Businesspeople take pride in destroying competitors, gaining more and more material possessions, and seeing fame and personal prosperity as the end result of the "pursuit of happiness."

The church often mirrors the culture in its definition of success. "Successful" churches have the most wealth, the greatest influence, the most power, and the greatest talent. The early church, however, defined success differently. Churches were successful by relying on the Holy Spirit's power, by suffering for the cause of Christ, and by maintaining unity and spreading the gospel in the face of imperial persecution.

In order to subvert the Caesar of Success, Christians must guard against a celebrity culture that erodes Christian community. Christians must see faithfulness to Christ and his church as the goal, not the means to greater influence and bigger size. Subversive churches unite with other like-minded churches instead of competing for their members. As Christians point to the Lord, the One from whom all good gifts flow, the Caesar of Success falls to its rightful place at the footstool of the King, who succeeded in his mission by embracing the cross.

The Caesar of Money

Another Caesar that holds enormous sway over a vast segment of the American population is the Caesar of Money. Jesus said,

"You cannot serve God and Mammon."[12] "Mammon," in Jesus' day, was a personified way of speaking of money. Two thousand years later, we still personify money with titles like "The Almighty Dollar"—a designation that speaks volumes about the power we expect money to wield. We pledge allegiance to this "Caesar" with sayings like "Money is power," "We've got to keep up with the Joneses," and "The one who dies with the most toys wins."

Early Christians subverted the economic empire of Rome by seeing themselves as managers of God's gifts and their money as a blessing to be shared. True Christianity is subversive of money—not in that it rejects all wealth and financial gain, but in that it refuses to allow money to become a dictator. True Christianity does not allow money to ascend to the throne of absolute power.

Churches can show that money is not lord by demonstrating to the world that all money comes from God, embracing a mind-set that focuses on eternal investments over temporal benefits, and showing the world that people matter more than possessions. The best way to subvert the idol of mammon is by giving it away freely. Communities of faith can do this by giving away a large percentage of offerings to other worthwhile mission efforts. The church should not be the end destination for tithes and offerings, but a funnel through which blessing can flow out to the world. These are ways we show the world that money is not the king . . . Jesus is.

The Caesar of Leisure

We will devote an entire chapter to discussing the proper place for leisure in our lives. Recreational activities make up part of what it means to be distinctly human. We can enjoy the fruits of our labor, admire beautiful art, soak up the glory of creation, and play sports and games for recreation. Yet, leisure is all too ready to leave its proper place in our lives and steal the throne. Instead of being a friend to a hard worker, leisure often morphs into a taskmaster that squeezes the life out of us.

Just as the early church rejected the addictive entertainment of the Roman games, subversive communities of faith will encourage believers to consciously monitor their media intake. In order to subvert the Caesar of Leisure, we must begin thinking seriously about our free time, structuring our time in order to show that God is our first priority, and focusing our leisure time on people instead of the newest distractions of our entertainment culture.

The Caesar of Sex

The United States has become a sexualized culture. Pornography generates billions of dollars every year, while enslaving countless people to the vice of voyeurism and perverting the normal expectations of sexual expression between men and women in marriage. Sex is used to sell just about everything—cars, books, magazines, even hamburgers and toothpaste! In the last fifty years, we have turned from a well-defined sexual morality to a sexual anarchy that has left broken families, abandoned children, abortion, and sexual addiction in its wake. "Free love" didn't turn out to be so free after all.

In the chapter on the Caesar of Sex, we will learn that sex is one of God's good gifts, a treasure that has its place within the marriage covenant. But the Caesar of Sex would have us enslaved to our sexual passions.

Christian communities can subvert the idol of sex in several ways. First, those who are single must commit to chastity (a life of purity), not merely abstinence. Secondly, we should celebrate sex within marriage, which means we will maintain a biblical understanding of marriage as a covenant. Third, we should be wary of our culture's attempts to separate sex from procreation. We will foster a church culture that celebrates large families and sees children as a gift from God. Lastly, we must work together to put up boundaries in our lives that will protect us from sexual temptation.

The Caesar of Power

Those who bow down to the Caesar of Power are quickly corrupted by the desire to obtain or maintain positions of authority. The early Christians realized that power could be a corrosive influence, so they devoted themselves to serving one another. Nothing puts power in its proper place more than service and sacrifice.

As we look at the biblical teaching of power and authority, we will see that power can only be used for good when it is placed at the feet of Jesus as the sovereign Lord. His power and authority was recognized *after* his descent into our world to be the Suffering Servant. He is our model.

Subversive churches share power, instead of concentrating it all in one place. We subvert power by seeing things from a kingdom perspective, meaning that true strength is often found in what seems to the world as weakness. Most importantly, we subvert power by using our authority as a way to benefit the lives of others. Instead of grappling for position and authority, we put others ahead of ourselves. If we were truly subversive of authority and power, our church parking lots would fill up from the back to the front.

WORLD-CHANGING CHRISTIANITY

If Jesus is King, then we should be spreading his influence into our world by taking up our crosses, denying ourselves, and showing that there is a different way to live: a way that subverts the Caesars of our world and exalts our risen Savior, and a way that provides a foretaste of the life to come, that is part of new creation spilling out, in, and over the old world that is passing away.

True Christianity is not merely *life*-changing; it is *world*-changing. Emphasize only the changing of individual lives and we will fail to call political systems, philosophies, and human structures to account under Jesus' lordship. Emphasize only political systems, philosophies, and human structures and we will compromise in our work for worldly progress while people remain dead in their sins. But put the message of Jesus' atoning death on the cross together with the biblical call to bring our world under the lordship of the risen Jesus and we have an explosive message that rocks our world to its very core. It is the apostolic message of Christianity.

True conversion manifests itself in our pledging allegiance to Jesus Christ as Lord and Savior, hence Paul's early formulation of the Christian creed: "Jesus is Lord and God raised him from the dead." Christianity hinges upon Jesus and what has happened to him *in history*. When we confess with our mouths that he is Lord, and believe in our hearts in his resurrection, we are saved.

Acts 17 records the results of this outward transformation:

> They dragged Jason and some of the brothers before the city authorities, shouting, "These men who have turned the world upside down have come here also, and Jason has received them, and they are all acting against the decrees of Caesar, saying that there is another king, Jesus." (Acts 17:6–7)

What if we heard these words again from those in our own generation? These Christians are turning the world upside down! They are acting against the Caesars of our day.

They are disobeying the Caesar of Success by praying for their competitors, making career choices that put family over finances, and seeking to be above reproach in their business practices.

They are dethroning the Caesar of Money by giving away their possessions and downsizing.

They are acting against the Caesar of Leisure and entertainment by sacrificing vacation time to go to foreign countries to help others who will never be able to return the favor.

They refuse to worship the Caesar of Sex and instead commit themselves to chastity, purity, and faithfulness in marriage for life.

They are acting against the Caesar of Power by modeling the self-giving love of their King.

And most of all, these Christians are saying there is another King—Jesus.

As Christians, we pledge allegiance to Jesus as King. We believe that Jesus, the Messiah of Israel who was crucified for our sins, has been raised from the dead and is now Lord of the universe. This means that we are to put our trust in his sacrifice and live submissively under his lordship.

It is not enough to think that salvation is a mere acceptance of a ticket to heaven that leaves the rest of our life intact. Salvation in Jesus Christ transforms lives. Life transformation leads to involvement in the church. When the community of those who have given allegiance to Jesus Christ lives in such a way as to quietly subvert the Caesars of the day, world transformation follows.

This is what it means to be a Christian.

SUBVERTING THE SELF

Three Strikes, You're Out

THE EARTH TURNS ON its orbit for you.

> The oceans ebb and flow for you.
> The birds sing for you.
> The sun rises and it sets for you.
> The stars come out for you . . .
> You are the master of the universe . . .
> You are the perfection of life . . . [1]

No, these are not the lyrics from the newest Hillsong worship CD. Neither do they come from the psalmist. These lines are taken from one of the best-selling books of 2007, Rhonda Byrne's *The Secret*, a publishing phenomenon that sold millions of copies in a short amount of time. Unfortunately, the lyrics of praise are not directed toward God, but to *you!* It used to be that people would frown upon the idea of acting as if the world revolves around you. Byrne turns that sentiment into a compliment.

Byrne's *The Secret* takes the power of positive thinking to a whole new level. If you want a good job, want to make more money, or want to have a better life, then all you have to do is think positive thoughts. You must expect the universe to conform to your demands and then be open to receiving what you desire.

Byrne's advice leads people to selfish behavior that can be frightening at times. For example, she suggests that one should avoid listening to people talk about their illnesses or problems because their negative thoughts might cause you to lose your positive energy. One should never sacrifice, either financially or personally. The self-sacrificial mind-set proves that you believe in lack and not abundance. Always put yourself first. Look out for your own interests ahead of everyone else's. After all:

> You are God in physical body. You are spirit in the flesh. You are a cosmic being. You are all power. You are all wisdom. You are the creator and you are creating a creation of you on this planet.[2]

We might be tempted to dismiss *The Secret* as being on the fringe of society. Most self-help books do not go to the extremes that Byrne advocates. But the fact that the book has become a bestseller should give us pause. And even a surface comparison of Byrne's teaching with that of many TV preachers will reveal distressing similarities. One such preacher defines the favor of God as finding a good parking spot or the ability to be near the front of a line.

Never mind Jesus' statements about the last being first and the first last. Never mind the idea that we should put others ahead of ourselves and do to them what we would have them do to us. Never mind the fact that Jesus said the greatest love is laying down your life for someone else. We are in love with ourselves, and we seek our own interests above all others. Nothing tempts us more than the desire to be in charge of our own destiny.

THE CAESAR OF SELF

The world constantly tells us that we are the center of the universe. Visit an online store and see how the advertising is tailored to what you have previously purchased or browsed. Look at the way products are marketed to our children. Listen to the pop songs encouraging us to "listen to your heart," "trust the voice within," and "believe in yourself."

The default setting for the human's outlook on life is self-centered. Do parents have to teach their children to be selfish? No. We are naturally self-centered. We think the world exists for us. We think our family exists for us. We think the church exists for us. And, ultimately, we look at salvation and see God himself as existing for us and for our glory.

Sociologist Christian Smith has done extensive research on the religious beliefs of American teenagers. He has found that the most common view of God among teenagers today likens him to a divine butler or a cosmic therapist. By and large, young people believe that "God exists to meet my needs."[3] God exists to help you become a better you by awakening the spark of life inside yourself. Both the biblical view of God's glory and the biblical purpose for human existence are languishing among most young people, including those in evangelical churches.

This mind-set is not new. The early Christians battled the influence of Gnosticism in the second, third, and fourth centuries. The Gnostics also believed that salvation was found in secret knowledge that came from special teachers. They taught that salvation came from within oneself. Rhonda Byrne and others stand in a long line of teachers who have espoused Gnostic-like teachings. And today, just as in previous periods of church history, we as Christians must subvert this Caesar we call The Self by proclaiming the biblical gospel.

To strike down the self and put it in its proper place, we must turn to the biblical teaching about salvation. The Bible teaches that salvation starts in the heart of God. The gospel is primarily about Jesus. Salvation is a gift of pure grace. And God has saved us in order for us to take part in a community of believers.

THE EPHESIANS ROAD

Some of the first Bible verses I ever memorized were from Paul's letter to the Romans. My Sunday school teachers equipped us to share the gospel with others by teaching us the "Romans Road." We were instructed in how to recite the verses in Romans that deal with personal sin and teach about the salvation found in the death and resurrection of Jesus Christ. I have found the Romans Road to be a helpful evangelistic strategy at times, but today, I prefer to turn to the first two chapters of Ephesians. Call it the "Ephesians Road" if you like.

The content of Paul's letter to Ephesus helps strike down the self-centered notions of humanity's "default setting" and puts forth a radically God-centered view of salvation and the world. Using a baseball analogy, I find in the first two chapters of Ephesians three strikes against the Caesar of Self.

Strike One

Salvation is about God's plan for the world, and the gospel is what he has done through Jesus of Nazareth in order to accomplish that plan (Ephesians 1).

Paul's opening lines portray God as the central figure and primary actor in the drama of salvation. In the original Greek, the following verses actually constitute one very long sentence. (Our English translations helpfully break the sentence up into several sentences to make reading easier.)

> Blessed be the God and Father of our Lord Jesus Christ, who has blessed us in Christ with every spiritual blessing in the heavenly places, even as he chose us in him before the foundation of the world, that we should be holy and blameless before him. In love he predestined us for adoption as sons through Jesus Christ, according to the purpose of his will, to the praise of his glorious grace, with which he has blessed

us in the Beloved. In him we have redemption through his blood, the forgiveness of our trespasses, according to the riches of his grace, which he lavished upon us, in all wisdom and insight making known to us the mystery of his will, according to his purpose, which he set forth in Christ as a plan for the fullness of time, to unite all things in him, things in heaven and things on earth. In him we have obtained an inheritance, having been predestined according to the purpose of him who works all things according to the counsel of his will, so that we who were the first to hope in Christ might be to the praise of his glory. In him you also, when you heard the word of truth, the gospel of your salvation, and believed in him, were sealed with the promised Holy Spirit, who is the guarantee of our inheritance until we acquire possession of it, to the praise of his glory. (Eph. 1:3–14)

Paul's introductory words to the Ephesians are radically God-centered. Salvation begins with God. He says our personal salvation begins with God choosing us before the foundation of the world, rescuing us by sending Jesus to die for our sins, and sealing us with the power of the Holy Spirit. Salvation also extends to the whole cosmos—the uniting of all things in Christ, things in heaven and things on earth. In another passage, Paul speaks of God being "all in all."[4] So the first strike against the self is to see how we fit in the overarching plan of God, not how God fits into our own vision of salvation.

"The Four Spiritual Laws" has been a popular evangelistic tool in recent years.[5] The first law is that "God loves you and has a wonderful plan for your life." There are two potential problems with this statement. First, God's "wonderful plan" for Christians may include times of suffering and persecution whereby we become more conformed to the image of Christ.[6]

A second problem is that this first law starts out by proclaiming what God has in store for us personally. The better, more biblical place to begin is to affirm that "God has a wonderful plan, period." Salvation is not primarily about God's plan for my life, but about God's renewal of everything. It is only within the vision of the glorious new world that God has promised that we find the strength to cope with the fact that God may have a very *difficult* plan for our lives.

If you have ever looked at the back side of a quilt or a tapestry, you see that there seems to be no overall design or pattern. The tapestry looks strange, without purpose or direction. But once you turn it over, you see how the individual patterns make up something that is beautiful.

Our lives do not always seem wonderful. But rather than trying to see what wonderful plan God has for giving us our best life now, Christians trust that the picture God is painting will be beautiful, so we look to experiencing our best life later.[7] God has a wonderful plan, and because of his grace, we are part of that plan.

Debtors to Grace

Once we recognize God's proper place at the center of salvation, we realize that we deserve nothing from him. Every aspect of our salvation comes to us purely by his grace. God has chosen to do something wonderful for us when we have done nothing to deserve mercy.

Christians have long debated whether or not God's election is based solely on his mercy or in his foreknowledge of future free decisions made by human beings. We can never fully understand the intricacies of how divine sovereignty and human responsibility coexist. I like the way the *Baptist Faith and Message* (2000) puts it:

> Election is the gracious purpose of God, according to which he regenerates, justifies, sanctifies, and glorifies sinners. It is consistent with the free agency of man, and comprehends

all the means in connection with the end. It is the glorious
display of God's sovereign goodness, and is infinitely wise,
holy, and unchangeable. It excludes boasting and promotes
humility.[8]

The doctrine of election rubs us the wrong way sometimes.
We like to be in control. We like to have our say. It runs against
our Western ideals of autonomy and independence to think that
our choice in salvation is dependent on God's choice of us before
the foundation of the world. We like to turn 1 John 4:19 on its
head and think that God loves us because we first loved him.

Have you ever wondered why God chose not to provide
redemption for the fallen angels? We are so prone to putting
ourselves in the center of God's plan for the world that we hardly
entertain the notion that God did not have to save *anyone*! Just
as he chose not to provide salvation for the angels who rebelled
against him, God was under no obligation to provide salvation
for humans. He would have been perfectly just to obliterate his
creation and begin anew.

But God, in his love and mercy, chose to save us—his image-
bearers. In fact, Scripture teaches that even the angels who did
not sin wish they could know and experience God's forgiveness
and redemption. Think about this fact for a moment: our salvation is the envy of angels![9]

Adopted by God

The apostle Paul turns to the analogy of adoption. My wife spent
several months one summer working with orphaned children in
Romania who had AIDS. Most of these children had contracted
HIV as babies. They had been brought to the doctor for vac-
cines and had received HIV from tainted needles instead. Most
were subsequently abandoned by their parents. With no hope

of adoption, these children were left with other AIDS-infected children to die in special orphanages.

No one adopts Romanian children with AIDS. They are left to die, to wither away with little love or care. Spiritually, we are in the same situation. We are orphans, in the clutches of sin and death. And yet, God has chosen to adopt us as his children. Even while we were still sinners, Christ died for us![10]

Adoption starts in the heart of the parent. A parent simply chooses a child and takes him or her home (the process takes a very long time, of course, but that is what ultimately takes place). Most adopted children are very young and have no say in the matter. They are on a path toward misery until someone from outside their world comes in and says, "I choose you."

Adoption is a beautiful picture of salvation. God has graciously chosen to adopt us, even though we were sin-infected orphans. He has chosen us according to the purpose of his will, to the praise of his glorious grace. He has adopted us and made us his children. He has given us the inheritance of new heavens and new earth promised in the Scriptures.

A Christ-centered Gospel

Salvation is not centered in the glory of some generic God, but in the God who has revealed himself to us in the person of Jesus Christ. Salvation's purpose is the glory of God *in Christ*. The next section of Ephesians 1 focuses on what Jesus Christ has accomplished.

> For this reason, because I have heard of your faith in the Lord Jesus and your love toward all the saints, I do not cease to give thanks for you, remembering you in my prayers, that the God of our Lord Jesus Christ, the Father of glory, may give you a spirit of wisdom and of revelation in the knowledge of him, having the eyes of your hearts enlightened, that

you may know what is the hope to which he has called you, what are the riches of his glorious inheritance in the saints, and what is the immeasurable greatness of his power toward us who believe, according to the working of his great might that he worked in Christ when he raised him from the dead and seated him at his right hand in the heavenly places, far above all rule and authority and power and dominion, and above every name that is named, not only in this age but also in the one to come. And he put all things under his feet and gave him as head over all things to the church, which is his body, the fullness of him who fills all in all. (Eph. 1:15–23)

The gospel of the early Christians was Christ-centered. The gospel is not a message about *us* (for example, "You are a sinner, and you need a Savior"). It is a message *for* us, yes. But it is first and foremost a message about Jesus Christ and what he has done, to the glory of God the Father.

A popular method of sharing the gospel today is giving testimony to the work of Jesus in your own life. Many evangelistic strategies center on the personal testimony as the most effective way of presenting the gospel. You simply speak about what your life was like before you trusted in Christ and what your life is like now that Christ has changed you.

Testimony-based evangelism can indeed be effective. The apostle Paul speaks of his Damascus road experience numerous times in the New Testament. The blind man in John 9 gives testimony to the healing power of Jesus, and the Samaritan woman in John 4 bears witness to Jesus' supernatural knowledge. Giving personal testimony has biblical precedent.

But let us not make the mistake of substituting testimony about Jesus (his life, death, and resurrection) with testimony about ourselves. We are not called to appeal to our subjective, spiritual experiences with Jesus when preaching the gospel. We are called to proclaim a message *about* Jesus, *for* sinners. In Ephesians 1, notice how the apostle Paul writes about what Jesus Christ has done. He appeals to historical events, not only here in Ephesians, but also in his sermons recorded in Acts and in his other letters.

If we are inclined to share our personal testimonies, so be it. But let us be sure to incorporate our own personal stories within the biblical story of Jesus. Our own testimonies are worth little if they do not include the historical truth claims that form the heart of the Christian faith. If we fail to preach Christ, we are leaving the self on the throne. We are giving testimony about ourselves, not God.

Paul tells us that God's plan is "to unite all things in him [Christ], things in heaven and things on earth."[11] Jesus has been raised from the dead and exalted "far above all rule and authority and power and dominion."[12] Jesus is ruling the world, not only in this age, but also in the one to come.

Salvation is not just about a new *you*, but a new *world*—a world in which you have been chosen to play a part. We trust in the God who has promised this new world, and we long eagerly for the day when Christ will return. Jesus instructs us to pray, "Your kingdom come, your will be done on earth as it is in heaven." In other words, *Lord, bring the rule of heaven here!* A song by Bob Kauflin says it well:

> Let your kingdom come,
> Let your will be done,
> So that everyone might know your name.
> Let your song be heard
> Everywhere on earth
> Till your sovereign work on earth is done
> Let your kingdom come.[13]

In Ephesians 1, we learn that salvation starts in the heart of God and that its purpose is the glory of God in Christ through our inheritance of the new earth that has been guaranteed by the Holy Spirit. We also learn about Jesus—that he has been raised from the dead, that he is the Lord of the world, and that he is the head of the church. Such wonderful news should cause us to rejoice from the very depths of our souls!

Charles Spurgeon, the famous preacher, said,

> It's not enough to hear about Jesus: Mere hearing may tune the harp, but the fingers of living faith must create the music. If you have seen Jesus with the God-giving sight of faith, suffer no cobwebs to linger among the harp-strings, but loud with the praise of sovereign grace, awake your psaltery and harp.[14]

Strike Two

Salvation comes only by the grace of God (Eph. 2:1–9).

The next truth strikes at the Caesar of Self by taking the implications of the gospel message about Jesus and showing us how that message affects us.

> And you were dead in the trespasses and sins in which you once walked, following the course of this world, following the prince of the power of the air, the spirit that is now at work in the sons of disobedience—among whom we all once lived in the passions of our flesh, carrying out the desires of the body and the mind, and were by nature children of wrath, like the rest of mankind. But God, being rich in mercy, because of the great love with which he loved us, even when we were dead in our trespasses, made us alive together with Christ—by grace you have been saved—and raised us up with him and seated us with him in the heavenly places in Christ Jesus, so that in the coming ages he

might show the immeasurable riches of his grace in kindness toward us in Christ Jesus. For by grace you have been saved through faith. And this is not your own doing; it is the gift of God, not a result of works, so that no one may boast. (Eph. 2:1–9)

Raised from the Dead

I have sometimes heard salvation described like this: *You're out in the ocean drifting away, sinking in your sins, flailing about, crying, "Save me! Help me!" A boat is nearby. Someone hears your cry for help and throws you a life raft. All you must do is cling to that life raft in faith to be reeled in and be saved.*

I doubt that Paul would have used such an illustration of salvation. Ephesians 2 indicates that, for Paul, there is no lost person who is flailing about, crying out for help. Paul does not give us a picture of a living person who is about to drown; in fact, he describes someone who is already dead. I believe Paul would describe salvation in a manner closer to this: *You are a floating corpse, face down, dead in the water, drowned in your trespasses and sins. Suddenly, someone yanks you out of the water, throws you down on the floor of the boat and gives you mouth-to-mouth resuscitation, breathing new life into you.*

Which rescue story is more impressive? Which story makes God look more glorious? A God who throws us a life raft and says, "Come on! I hope you make it!" or a God who resurrects the person who has already drowned?

Paul's description of our life before Christ is bleak. We are the "living dead," physically alive, but spiritual corpses, carrying out our evil desires. Paul not only tells us that we were dead; he also claims that we were "children of wrath"—people who deserve punishment.

Saved from God's Wrath

One of the world's most beloved hymns is "Amazing Grace," written by John Newton, a man who had once captained slave ships, but who had been transformed by the grace of God. *Amazing grace! How sweet the sound that saved a wretch like me!*

Pastor Robert Schuller has protested the words of "Amazing Grace." He encourages people to alter the first verse so that it says, *How sweet the sound that saved a* soul *like me.* Another variation could be, *How sweet the sound that saved and* strengthened *me.* Many artists who cover the song follow Schuller's suggestions. The original seems too condemning, too humiliating, too shameful. How can we see ourselves as wretched before God, deserving his wrath?

Speaking about God's wrath today is very unpopular, just as it has been for centuries. How do you reconcile the biblical image of a God of love with the biblical teaching about God's wrath? It is unfortunate that some theologians and pastors set up such a strong distinction between God's judgment and love. In some theologies, God appears to be bipolar! We should avoid setting God's attributes against one another.

Instead, it is better to understand that God's wrath is based on his love. God so loved the world that he sent his Son. God loves this world too much to let it go on the way it is. He has promised to punish sin and purge the evil from the world, bringing justice and everlasting peace.

As humans made in God's image, we experience a longing for justice that is knit into our very being. We want to see evildoers judged. We want to see justice enacted. When we see people close to us being abused by others, our love for them causes us to be rightfully wrathful against those who would harm them.

Suppose there is a man who has been found guilty of child

molestation. He goes before the judge and asks for his sentence to be commuted.

The judge asks, "Are you sorry?"

The man replies, "Yes. I'm very sorry."

So the judge says, "Then, you do not have to go jail. You can go home."

We would be right to demand that judge's resignation. We would be right to expose the fact that the judge is not ruling justly. And yet, many people picture God as that type of judge. We think to ourselves, "I will work it out with God later. God will let me off. After all, he loves me." We desire justice in the world, that evildoers be punished, and that perpetrators be caught and held accountable for their crimes; and yet we hypo-critically refuse to see our own contributions to the evil of the world, or the magnitude of our own sinful rebellion against God!

We want God to act fairly and justly, to purge the world of evil and bring about his peaceful reign. But when we realize that the line of evil runs through each one of us, we begin to understand that God cannot purge the world of evil and save "a wretch like me"—unless, of course, he acts mercifully and justly by taking upon himself our own condemnation.

God's Intervention to Save Us

In Ephesians 2, Paul says, "You are dead. You deserve God's wrath." But then everything changes with two words: *But God.* "But God, being rich in mercy . . . made us alive together with Christ."[15] God has sent his Son to live the perfect life that we could never live and then to die as our substitute—to bear the wrath of God that we deserved in order that we might be a part of the new world that he is creating.

Why has God acted in such a way? Paul gives two reasons. First, God has saved us because he loves us. In fact, Paul says that God's love for us is great. But there is another reason why God has chosen to save us: to show the immeasurable riches of his grace in kindness toward us in Christ Jesus. If we were to translate this concept into the vernacular, it would be something like this: God has saved you in order to show off his grace.

We seek to avoid the quality of "showing off." But with God, what else can he praise? What else is there to shine a spotlight on? What is more glorious than what God has done for us in Christ Jesus?

Salvation starts in the heart of God. The gospel centers on Jesus. Salvation is a gift that comes from God's great love for us, so that he might be able to show the world how gracious he is. Again and again, Paul tells us in Ephesians that salvation is all of God, all from God, and all for God.

The gospel message subverts the self. It reminds us that we are not the center of the universe; God is. We are not the focus of the gospel message; Jesus is. We do not in any way earn our salvation; God has done it all.

Nothing cuts us down to size like the cross of Christ. John Stott says,

> Every time we look at the cross, Christ seems to say to us, "I am here because of you. It is your sin I am bearing, your curse I am suffering, your debt I am paying, your death I am dying." Nothing in history or in the universe cuts us down to size like the cross.[16]

Strike Three

Salvation comes with a calling that must be fulfilled within the community of faith (Eph. 2:10–22).

I have spoken with many people who believe they are true Christians, and yet they see no need for the local church. Once I probe a little deeper into their understanding of salvation, I find a truncated view of redemption that is highly individualistic ("It's all about me and Jesus!") and often centered on the benefits of a heavenly afterlife ("I've prayed the prayer and have my ticket to heaven!").

But once I analyze the gospel presentations that these people have heard, I can hardly fault them. The disciples we produce are a direct result of the gospel we preach.[17] If we proclaim a gospel that focuses only on the private experience of the individual and the heavenly benefits for the next life, then we should not be surprised to see people dismissing the importance of good works in this life within the context of the church.

Destined for Good Works

The rest of Ephesians 2 is vitally important if we are to cut the legs out from under the Caesar of Self and see the self fall back to its proper place, at the feet of Jesus the King. For Paul, salvation has a communal aspect that has a distinctly outward orientation.

> For we are his workmanship, created in Christ Jesus for good works, which God prepared beforehand, that we should walk in them. (Eph. 2:10)

Paul says that not only have the benefits of our salvation been prepared beforehand by God, but also the good works that come from our salvation. We are destined to do good works.

There are two kinds of Christians. "Sink Christians" view salvation as they would a sink. The water of salvation flows into the sink so that Christians can soak up all the benefits: eternal life, assurance in the presence of God, and strength in times of trial. Those who adopt this mind-set concentrate solely on what the Bible says God has done and will do for them.

"Faucet Christians" view salvation differently. They look at the world as the sink and themselves as the faucet. The blessings of salvation flow *to* them in order to flow *through* them out to the wider world. They rightly see that the Bible describes salvation as something that God not only does for them, but also through them.

Abraham was chosen not only to receive God's blessing, but also so that the nations might be blessed through him.[18] Likewise, God blessed Joseph by placing him in a powerful position of authority in Egypt, and Joseph used his position to save the nation of Egypt (and his own family as well).[19] Israel was chosen to be the light of the world, not only to receive God's light (Jesus said they should not hide it under a bowl, keeping it to themselves[20]), but to reflect God's light so that the peoples living in darkness would see God's glory.[21]

Do you see? God has not merely chosen us in order that we might enjoy the benefits of new creation. He has chosen us to be vessels through which new creation spreads into the world. We are called to proclaim salvation to the nations, and to be a blessing to the people around us. We were predestined not only for heaven, but also for earth! We were predestined by God to do good works. Seven times in Paul's letter to Titus, he commands him to "do good" to all.

As a teenager in the late 1990s, I felt an ever-increasing burden for the people in formerly Communist Eastern European countries. In 2000, when I was nineteen years old, I bought a one-way ticket to Romania and made that country my home and place of education and ministry for five years.

During the summer of 2001, I spent a few months at home in the U.S. After September 11, many people recommended that I put off my Romanian mission work and wait a month or two in the United States. I felt compelled to fly back to Romania anyway, even if it meant leaving just seven days after the terrorist attacks, and even if it meant I would make a connection in Washington, the airport in which terrorists had boarded the plane that crashed into the Pentagon.

The Sunday night before I was to leave, a godly lady in my church encouraged me to lean on Ephesians 2:10. She said, "You have nothing to fear, Trevin. You are part of God's workmanship, created in Christ Jesus for good works, which God prepared beforehand. You are invincible until you have done all the good works that God has destined for you to do." And then she added with a smile, "I don't think God is through with you yet."

Ephesians 2:10 gave me comfort during those difficult days. Of course, we never know when we will take our last breath. But even in perilous times, we can rest in the sovereignty of God who has prepared good works for us to do. Our good works are essential to salvation, not because they earn us favor with God, but because they *prove* our identity as God's children by putting on display God's majesty, God's love, and God's gospel.

Intended for the Kingdom Community

Ephesians 2 begins by speaking of our individual salvation and the good works we are to do. But the rest of the chapter shows how salvation's aim is to incorporate us into a kingdom community.

> Therefore remember that at one time you Gentiles in the flesh, called "the uncircumcision" by what is called the circumcision, which is made in the flesh by hands—remember that you were at that time separated from Christ, alienated from the commonwealth of Israel and strangers to the covenants of promise, having no hope and without God in the world. But now in Christ Jesus you who once were far off have been brought near by the blood of Christ. For he himself is our peace, who has made us both one and has broken down in his flesh the dividing wall of hostility by abolishing the law of commandments expressed in ordinances, that he

might create in himself one new man in place of the two, so making peace, and might reconcile us both to God in one body through the cross, thereby killing the hostility. And he came and preached peace to you who were far off and peace to those who were near. For through him we both have access in one Spirit to the Father. So then you are no longer strangers and aliens, but you are fellow citizens with the saints and members of the household of God, built on the foundation of the apostles and prophets, Christ Jesus himself being the cornerstone, in whom the whole structure, being joined together, grows into a holy temple in the Lord. In him you also are being built together into a dwelling place for God by the Spirit. (Eph. 2:11–22)

Jesus did not die merely to save us as individuals; he died to purchase a church—people from every tribe, tongue, and nation. The church is not an afterthought in the purposes of God. Church attendance is more than simply the fine print at the bottom of our gospel presentations, a good work we tell people to do after they come to faith. Understanding the role of the church is central if we are to strike down the Caesar of Self.

The church is central in God's purposes for the world. Christ is our peace. He has made Jew and Gentile one and has "broken down in his flesh the dividing wall of hostility." God is not merely giving individuals new life; he is forming them into the church which is "growing into a holy temple in the Lord."

It is popular today to adopt the mind-set that "Jesus is great, but the church is terrible." People may say, "I love Jesus, but I can't stand the church." Paul uses two metaphors about the church. In one, he says that the church is Christ's body.[22] In another, he says that the church is Christ's bride.[23] For someone to say "I love Jesus, but I can't stand the church" is like me telling my wife, "I love you, Corina, but I can't stand your body!"

Though the church is filled with many imperfections, she remains central to the purposes of God. For all of her problems, the church is still the place where the glorious symphony of the gospel of Jesus is played most beautifully.

Reflecting God to the World

Paul points out the ramifications of the gospel for the church. Jesus Christ is Lord of the whole world, Jew and Gentile alike. We are united by the gospel, no matter our cultural backgrounds, social status, ethnicity, or race. In the church, people from all walks of life come together to form one body.

It is important that local churches seek to reflect the kingdom of God. We too quickly segregate our church members based on age, gender, or even musical preference! Some segregation might be helpful and practical at times (especially in areas of discipleship), but we should guard against spending all of our time at church with people just like us. Our churches should be multigenerational. Seniors in high school should be able to sit next to senior citizens and praise God with the same songs. We should be seeking to break down walls between generations, races, and nationalities.

The atonement brings about a community of believers. Once our churches divide into factions, according to social status, musical style, or ethnicity, we are unintentionally proclaiming to the world that something other than the cross of Jesus Christ unites us. We are showing people that what truly unites us is our musical preference, our race, our age, or our social class—not Christ.

Jesus died to reconcile us to God and to one another. We can offer inspiring worship services, but if everyone attending looks just like me and likes everything that I like, it could be that we are denying the gospel by implying that something else is at the center of our life and faith other than Jesus Christ and his cross and resurrection.

It is unfortunate that our churches spend so much time and energy in building up the very walls that Jesus died to tear down.

Paul's emphasis on the community of faith strikes at the heart of the self. We are to crucify our own desires and put others ahead of ourselves. The place we do this is in the local congregation. How often do we die to ourselves for the church? How often do we put aside our own preferences for the benefit of others?

The church should subvert the world's way of thinking. Only in a church of Jesus Christ can a teenager go into a class of senior adult ladies (some of whom have been walking with Jesus for fifty years) and hear a lady ask, "What can you teach us?" Only in the church can a poor man with no high school education teach a Bible study that may have a rich man with a PhD in attendance!

CONCLUSION

The Ephesians Road strikes out the self and places it in its proper place. Strike one takes place when we see that salvation starts with God and the gospel message is all about Jesus. Strike two occurs when we realize that salvation is all of God's grace and we have nothing to contribute. Strike three happens when we understand that God has saved us in order to place us in a community of faith that will be a blessing to the nations.

The salvation of God is *for* us. The Father has chosen us. Jesus' blood has purchased us. We are adopted orphans.

Salvation is *to* us. The Holy Spirit stirs our heart, so that we come to faith in Jesus Christ personally. We are forgiven sinners.

Salvation is also *through* us. The world will be blessed by the good deeds we do in the context of the community of faith. We are commissioned communities.

SUBVERTING SUCCESS

Finding Success in Our Suffering

AT A WELL-KNOWN SEMINARY, a recent poll asked students what they hoped to do after their academic career had ended and they had begun their service in local churches. A large majority of students indicated that they hoped to serve in a church within 90 miles of family and friends. Most indicated a desire to live in the city or suburbs—someplace where shopping malls and supermarkets were easily accessible. Many mentioned the price range of the comfortable home they hoped to own—a big house with a couple of cars in the garage. In short, students wanted successful ministries where they could serve the church without sacrificing personal comfort.

As I considered the results from the informal poll, I was struck by how closely the answers resembled the hopes and dreams of society at large. Ask a handful of college students at any secular university the same questions and you will receive the same answers. Comfort. Pleasure. Success.

The results from the seminary poll should haunt us. Should Christian leaders have the same vision of success as the world around us? What is "success" anyway?

VISIONS OF SUCCESS

The world's definition of success has not changed much in the past two-thousand years. In ancient Rome, three factors determined your success in life: citizenship, prosperity, and security. Only an elite few had all three. Most of the people in ancient Rome didn't have any. For the poor, "success" was defined as another meal. Highly ambitious slaves might work off their debts and then align themselves with the wealthy to ensure a measure of security. But for most people in the Roman Empire, success remained elusive. Those who were considered "successful" embraced a life of hedonism that never satisfied their cravings.

Success in the twenty-first century is not all that different from ancient Rome. The majority of Americans still see influence, class, and wealth as "success." The vision of successful business looms large over American society. We believe that we hold the keys to the successful life in our own hands, and so we dedicate most of our life to its pursuit.

Ancient Romans offered sacrifices to the gods and gave tribute to Rome in honor of the emperor. Today's Americans offer more costly sacrifices to the Caesar of Success. We sacrifice our health, even our families, in our pursuit of success. The business world is rife with animal metaphors that should give us pause: the "dog-eat-dog" business climate that casts off all ethical restraint in reaching the top, a "rat race" in which we must "claw" our way to the "front of the pack." There is something inherently dehumanizing about devoting one's life to the world's vision of success, and our vocabulary should clue us in that the obsessive pursuit of *more* success is *less* than what God intends.

THE CHURCH'S VIEW OF SUCCESS

Too often, the church mirrors the business world when it comes to defining success. "Buildings, budgets, and baptisms," the old adage goes. "Successful" churches are marked by a stream of wealth flowing into the ministry and a fast-growing number of constituents. Pastors and church leaders are under incredible pressure to do whatever it takes to see growth.

Imagine interviewing for a church position today and saying, "I believe God wants us to be kingdom-focused and mission-minded. It could be that as we start to move into more intensive discipleship, we will shrink before we grow." In most churches, you would be shown the door quickly. It's too risky. No one wants to hear about shrinking. Never mind that the concept is biblical. Never mind that Jesus talks about branches being pruned for the good of the tree.[1] Never mind that shrinking actually happened in Jesus' earthly ministry.[2] Embracing the small over the big? This is the era of super-sizing everything. Bigger is better—always; isn't it?

Our churches are parroting the surrounding culture's definitions of success. We have consumers (the congregation), a board of directors (deacons or elders), and a pastor CEO that we hire to give us results. Success is getting people in the door. Traffic. Marketing. Visibility. One of the reasons why some young people in their twenties have abandoned the church is that corporate-style Christianity is just a poor imitation of what we see in the world. It's what we get everywhere else.

Consider what happened to the early church after Constantine legalized Christianity in AD 313 and made it the state religion. Freedom was granted to the churches. Christianity suddenly found itself with all the worldly success it could ever dream of, including legitimization by the emperor himself. Yet, most church historians believe that this moment of "success" actually undermined the church and rendered it spiritually impotent in the face of newfound imperial power.

The church in the West is booming on a financial and social level. There are more churches now in the United States than ever before in our history. The percentage of people attending church weekly continues to hold steady. Buildings. Budgets. Baptisms. We have them all. But the influence of Christianity on American society is waning. Our impact is hardly felt. Could it be that we have finally reached the pinnacle of worldly "success" and this Caesar is undermining our witness?

FAITHFULNESS IS SUCCESS

During my time in Romania, I sat at the feet of a well-respected evangelical professor who had suffered persecution under the Communists. His father had been murdered by the Securitate in a car wreck that was made to look like an accident. This professor also served as a pastor of a local church. One day in class, he put aside his notes and began to speak heart-to-heart about pastoring.

"Brothers," he said, his voice quivering as he fought back tears, "Don't think that true success will come from adopting a strategy that will lead you to fulfilling one purpose. Jesus called himself the Good Shepherd—the One who lays down his life for his sheep. Success in God's eyes does not come without sacrifice. Don't try to be successful. Expend your energy in seeking to be faithful. Faithfulness *is* success."

SUBVERTING SUCCESS

I am often tempted to embrace the world's vision of success. I find my worth and value in what I can produce. Even when I know in my head that true success comes by remaining faithful, I find it difficult to accept that truth in my heart. I sometimes get depressed or feel like I'm failing if the class I teach on Sunday mornings has a week in which attendance is low.

In these moments of temptation to adopt worldly standards of success, I think back to the scene in John 18 where Jesus is standing before Pilate. The contrast between the world's kingdom and God's kingdom has never been clearer. Here stood the kingdom of man, propelled by the military force and imperial might of the Roman Empire. Yet there in the palace of human pride and ambition was the kingdom of God, whose innocent King faced the mockery and punishment reserved for lawbreakers. This King would reign by being lifted up on a Roman cross to suffer the punishment brought on by the sin of his people and, ultimately, the world.

The Caesars ruled by conquering. Jesus ruled by being conquered.

The Caesars ruled by might and brute force. Jesus ruled by laying down his life as a sacrifice for human sin.

The Caesars stayed in power by punishing those who rebelled. Jesus overcame the forces of sin and death by taking upon himself the punishment for rebellion.

If we are to subvert the Caesar of Success in today's world, we must follow the example of Christ, as did the early church. There are three ways that the Christian community can most visibly subvert this insidious Caesar: by recognizing that success is found in the Holy Spirit's power, by embracing suffering, and by pursuing unity.

Relying on the Spirit's Power Instead of Our Own

A church that understands the kingdom vision of success knows that success is not in its own hands. Our culture tells us that we are the makers of our future. We create our destiny. When this mind-set is applied to the church, the Spirit's role in bringing growth and maturity is minimized. The first subversion of the Caesar of Success is recognizing that only the Spirit's power brings lasting fruit.

The early church constantly relied on the Holy Spirit's power. The apostle Paul claimed that his "success" did not come from his talents and abilities but as a "demonstration of the Spirit and of power, that your faith might not rest in the wisdom of men but in the power of God."[3] For Paul, success without full reliance on the Holy Spirit was an idol that threatened the basis of faith.

In Acts, Luke follows the same pattern of thought in his description of the early church. As the first believers devoted themselves to prayer and fellowship, Luke tells us that "the *Lord* added to their number day by day those who were being saved."[4] Likewise, Luke continually reminds his readers that the Holy Spirit was the One who filled the apostles as they preached, led the missionaries as they went, and stirred repentance in the hearts of the hearers.

Today's church growth movement may be motivated by a sincere passion to see people come to faith in Christ. But one of the dangerous facets of this movement is the idea that you are in control. If you change your music, update your style, or build a new building, *you* can grow *your* church. *You* bring success. When the church adopts this mind-set, it has already succumbed to the prevailing notions of success in the culture.

Subversion of this subtle but powerful Caesar can occur only when the church places its complete trust in the power of the Spirit. The kingdom of God challenges our man-made efforts at achieving true success.

Embracing Suffering over Comfort

The second way to subvert the Caesar of Success is by rethinking our definition of success. Instead of agreeing with the world's definition of success (comfort, luxury, stability, wealth), we must redefine it according to the vision of the kingdom of God. Once we immerse ourselves in the biblical narrative of the kingdom, our imaginations are free to envision a different type of success, and we quickly discover that the kingdom vision of success includes the embrace of suffering as a means of becoming more like Christ.

The early Christians embraced suffering, torture, even martyrdom, because they knew that their sufferings gave them the opportunity to best proclaim the gospel message. Early Christians could not evangelize through public crusades and evangelistic rallies. The one place you could get a public hearing for the gospel was in a trial for martyrdom. That is why the church father Tertullian could say, "The blood of the martyrs is the seed of the church."[5] The intentional embrace of suffering preached volumes to a world dulled and desensitized by its own pursuit of success.

My father-in-law was a member of the Communist party in Romania during the 1970s. During that period of history, the Communists were the elite. They were ensured food, wealth, honor, and power. One night in 1974, the Communist party sent him to spy on a clandestine evangelical church service. He was to attend the service and report back to the party the names of those who were involved. But that night, the preacher's message gripped him: "Jesus is Lord." For the first time in his life, my father-in-law realized that the propaganda of the Communist regime was a sham. All rulers and powers and authorities, including the Romanian dictator, were subject to the Messiah crucified for our sins and raised for our salvation.

Family and friends tried to talk my father-in-law out of his newfound faith. Didn't he know he would sacrifice personal comfort for himself and his family? Didn't he know that he would lose all the respect he had in the Party? Didn't he know that he could be put in jail? What kind of kingdom would ask you to give up the trappings of "success" in exchange for a life of suffering? His answer echoed the words of Paul: "I consider that the sufferings of this present time are not worth comparing with the glory that is to be revealed to us."[6] Today he is a pastor, and the Lord has used him greatly over the years.

Success That Focuses on Others

The conscious, intentional embrace of suffering is the most subversive way to strike at the heart of the Caesar of Success. In a free society, we may not face the same kinds of persecution as in the early church or in Communist Romania. But that does not mean that the Caesar of Success is not alive and well today. If the nature of this Caesar is more subtle than expected, our subversion of this Caesar will also be subtle.

We subvert the Caesar of Success whenever we, as a community of faith, reject the idea that bigger is necessarily better.

We subvert success when we go from riches to rags on behalf of the world's poor rather than finding our hope in moving from rags to riches.

We subvert success when we find happiness and contentment in people, not things.

We subvert success when we intentionally live below our means in order to have more to give to the needy.

We subvert success when our churches partner with one another, not as competitors, but as coworkers in the kingdom.

We subvert success as businesspeople when we are willing to downsize, to take pay cuts in order to spend more time with family, or to refuse a promotion that would sacrifice church and family ties.

We subvert success by praying for our competitors' success and by thanking God for the success achieved by others, just as the early church prayed for the governing authorities who were persecuting them.

A Résumé of Suffering

Jesus' upside-down kingdom should flip our way of thinking. And that is why every time I need to update my résumé, I can't help but wonder if maybe I have gone about citing my accomplishments the wrong way. Followers of Jesus boast not in their strengths, but in their weaknesses.

In 2 Corinthians 11, Paul fills out a résumé that completely goes against what anyone would expect. No self-respecting Roman or Jew would have seen this list as one of accomplishment.

In Paul's day, when Roman armies attacked a city, the soldiers either forced the gate or used ladders to hurdle the wall. Of course, the enemy threw down anything and everything (rocks, boiling oil, etc.) to prevent the invaders from gaining entry. Just making it over the wall and into the city demonstrated a truly heroic feat. The first soldier to accomplish this death-defying act of bravery would receive the *corona muralis* ("the crown of the wall").

In Paul's upside-down résumé, we read about the time he managed to go over the city wall. However, in his case, he wasn't victoriously entering the city to claim it for the King. Rather, he was fleeing the city, under the cover of darkness, by being lowered over the wall in a basket. Here is the great apostle Paul, frightened and cowering in a basket, hoping to escape from the city before being caught and executed.

Paul's self-written letter of recommendation continues, but he doesn't boast of his accomplishments. He cites beatings, shipwrecks, public humiliation, imprisonment, and the time God seemingly abandoned him to drift in the sea for a whole day and night. He speaks of the dangers posed by fellow Jews, Christian hypocrites, and common thieves. He mentions exhaustion, hunger, and poverty. Is this the victorious Christian life that God promised? Where is his list of achievements? Where is his sense of pride from all that God has done through him?

If his letter of recommendation is going to convince the Corinthians that he is a true apostle and that the "apostles" who are disturbing the church are indeed false, then he'd better come up with a more impressive résumé than this! After all, if he's going to assert his apostolic authority, he had better prove to his people that he's a true apostle.

And somehow, that's the whole point. Paul lists his weaknesses, hardships, and failures in order to prove that he is a true apostle and the "super-apostles" handing out more impressive letters of recommendation are in fact the fakes. Being a follower of Jesus and a citizen of his upside-down kingdom means that what would normally be held up as worthy of praise and proof of authority is struck down, and what would normally be considered shameful and proof of failure is raised up in its place.

Of course, Paul is just following Jesus. The Messiah of Israel faced temptation in the wilderness, agonized over his future while suffering in the garden, and burst into tears before making his grand entrance into Jerusalem. The King of Israel did receive a crown—one full of thorns that only added to the agony and shame of Roman crucifixion, the most embarrassing and revolting form of execution ever devised.

Ultimately, it is the cross that turns the world's wisdom upside down and redefines our notions of success. We Christians hold up that ancient form of torture as our most beloved symbol of victory. It was in his excruciating death that Jesus was reconciling the world to God. It was in the suffering and the lashes of Roman whips that Paul was putting on display God's gospel for the world to see. It is in our weaknesses and sufferings that God's strength becomes crystal clear.

Followers of Christ should not equate success with a list of merits on a page. The marks of our Savior were nail scars in his hands and feet. The mark of the apostle was the whip-induced tearing of the flesh on the back. The mark of Jesus' follower is the suffering one endures after taking up the cross and following after him.

Why should we forget that following Christ means *going his way*? The crown that interested Paul wasn't the "crown of the wall" awarded by the Roman generals, but the crown of Christ, the reward from the crucified and risen Lord of the world. Somehow, it is through our suffering, our shame, our weakness and seeming failures that God makes visible the image of his Son.

When set against the backdrop of Christ's sufferings, our petty visions of success are unmasked for what they are: superficial and self-centered. The church has too often failed to live in such a way that our actions would stand the world's wisdom and thought processes on their head—the kingdom way—the upside-down, or should we say, *right-side-up* way that Jesus lived. We follow Christ when we stop showing off earthly crowns of "success" and embrace the crown of thorns that truly models the life of the Savior.

Pursuing Unity Instead of Sameness

One of the ways that the church has grown "successful" today has been through the adoption of ideas such as "the homogeneous principle." In short, this principle teaches that the way to build a church is to find a niche you want to market to, plant a church that reaches one type of people, fill the church with people who are the same, and watch it grow.

Is that success? Is a church of one-thousand members with a celebrity pastor, great programs and activities, and an exclusively white congregation successful? Most tend to think so.

But we need to let Scripture challenge us here. What are we compromising in our effort to bring together a church of people just like us? If the gospel is simply about individuals and a ticket to heaven, then we have missed nothing that is essential to the gospel. But if the gospel is bigger than that—if it includes the proclamation of Jesus as Lord of all (including all races, genders, nationalities, classes, etc.)—then perhaps in our "success" we are compromising an integral part of the gospel itself.

Much of the New Testament contains instruction about how to maintain unity in the body of Christ among the different ethnicities and cultures. The gospel is not merely about individual human beings being reconciled to God, but also about God creating a kingdom community, reconciling people to himself and to each other—people from different races, cultures, and ethnicities kneeling before the cross of Christ.

Paul commands us to eagerly pursue "the unity of the Spirit in the bond of peace."[7] Unity matters. In a postmodern society that sees fragmentation as one of the ways to increase economic success and marketing viability, Christians must consciously reach out to those from diverse backgrounds and cultures. When we begin intentionally inviting people who are different from us to our fellowship, we are signaling to the world that the kingdom understanding of success differs from the world's perspective.

A prominent Baptist church in the deep South saw numerical success in the 1980s and 1990s. Several years ago, a new pastor arrived and realized that the community was changing. Seventy-six percent of the community was nonwhite, but the church did not reflect the diversity. So, the new pastor led the church to begin reaching out to the different cultures around them. Soon, the church was having fourteen weekly worship services in nine languages. The church began working to impact the community for the kingdom. They opened a free medical clinic to treat the sick in the community who had no insurance. They opened a food pantry for the needy. They began teaching immigrants

English. They taught citizenship classes and business skills. They offered counseling for families in crisis.

Most importantly, this church undergirded all their good works with a strong emphasis on preaching the gospel and evangelizing the lost. As a result, they started seeing people come to faith in Christ. The church stopped measuring success based solely on weekly attendance numbers and began looking at the transformation of human lives.

During this time, the senior pastor received an anonymous letter that accused him of turning their great, historic church into a "soup kitchen." The following Sunday, the pastor read that letter to the congregation and then said, "That's *exactly* what we're doing."

The church became so involved in the community that they were bringing in people who did not have the financial resources to sustain the church. Any business that goes out and recruits customers that cannot pay is risking the welfare of the company. But this church trusted God for the resources and decided "success" was more than budgets, buildings, and baptisms. Granted, the church has big budgets, buildings, and baptisms. But they were driven by a kingdom-minded vision of success, not a worldly one.

Several times a year, all these different groups and nationalities come together for a church-wide Communion service held in nine different languages. The racial and ethnic unity envisioned by this church is deeply subversive of most church models of success. This church embodies the reality that Christians are from all tribes and nations. A united, peace-loving church is deeply subversive and deeply satisfying. It touches on what the gospel is, because it incarnates the message that Jesus is Lord of all.

Christians are former enemies pulled together by the cross of Jesus Christ. That is our foundation. We should not look for other commonalities or differences. We should be characterized by a pursuing love that envisions the unity we have as the family of God.

PURSUING FAITHFULNESS

Christian communities subvert the Caesar of Success when they recognize the Holy Spirit's power over results, redefine "success" to include the embrace of suffering, and actively pursue unity in the body of Christ. Each of these can be summed up as the pursuit of faithfulness. Christians are not called to be "successful"; we are called to be faithful.

The early church did not concentrate on growing the body of Christ numerically. They focused on being the body of Christ, and the Holy Spirit increased their number. The early Christians focused on living out the law of love and peace by being faithful to the crucified and risen Lord. They strived to make their fellowships the center of life and love. They defended the truth of the gospel over against the various heresies of paganism and Gnosticism. They concentrated on preserving the gospel message and handing down to the next generation what had been handed to them. They sought to create a place where God's love was made visible, and where the message of Jesus' lordship could be seen and entered.

This late second-century letter to Diognetus sums up the early Christian understanding of success and faithfulness:

> Christians do not find happiness by ruling over their neighbors, or by seeking supremacy over the weak, or by being rich, or by attacking the inferior. On the contrary, Christians see success in taking upon themselves the burdens of their neighbor, using their positions of superiority to benefit the deficient, and in distributing whatever they receive from God to the needy. *This* is what it means to be an imitator of God.

SUBVERTING MONEY

Taking "Almighty" off the Dollar

RIDE DOWN THE STREETS of the wealthiest counties in my home state, and you will see sprawling homes, multi-car garages, and a growing number of self-storage facilities. A story in *The Tennessean* featured a family with a 4,200-square-foot home who uses storage facilities for their "clutter," items that include big-screen TVs, an extra washer and dryer, and several pieces of furniture that haven't been "worked into the house yet." One of the storage facility managers was asked why his business is successful, and he replied: "People are narcissistic, materialistic. They can't part with their stuff."[1]

THE PURSUIT OF WEALTH

In the United States, we believe we have the right to life, liberty, and the pursuit of happiness. For the average American today, the pursuit of happiness *is* the pursuit of wealth. We even give money a blasphemous personification—"The Almighty Dollar"—a title that should be reserved for Almighty God. Jesus famously said, "You cannot serve God and Money."[2] ("Money" can also be translated "mammon," which was the personification that people in New Testament times gave to money.)

We justify our greed and covetousness by turning our consumerism into competition with our neighbors. "We've got to keep up with the Joneses," we say. We plaster our materialism on our cars through bumper stickers that reduce life to the accumulation of wealth: "The one who dies with the most toys wins!"

Also popular today is the phrase "Money is power." Taking into consideration Jesus' warnings about the seductiveness of mammon, I believe he would agree that "money is power," or at least *a* power—one of the powers and principalities that too quickly seek to take over the throne of our lives.

THE CAESAR OF MONEY

Money is given to us by God. Like all the Caesars mentioned in this book, wealth is not inherently evil. Some of the heroes of the Gospels were wealthy. Many Old Testament saints were blessed with financial prosperity. Money is a good gift from God.

Yet we face the persistent temptation to put money in the place of God, where it then becomes an idol. That's why the apostle Paul can say "the love of money is a root of all kinds of evils."[3] The Bible certainly displays the evil results that spring from the love of money. Greed and envy caused Cain to murder his brother Abel.[4] Achan's greed plunged Israel into the bloody battle of Ai, in which many Israelite soldiers lost their lives.[5] When money takes the throne as Caesar, the power of the coin begins to control our lives. We sacrifice anything and everything for money when it is our god.

At the time of this writing, a popular television game show is *The Moment of Truth*. In the show, a man or woman is hooked up to a lie detector and required to truthfully answer a series of increasingly personal and compromising questions. As the financial stakes get higher, the contestants show they are willing to sacrifice their closest relationships for the coolness of the coin. When money is our idol, we offer sacrifices to it.

The desire for money can bring out the worst in people. The biggest shopping day of the year is usually the day after

Thanksgiving, often called "Black Friday." In 2008, Black Friday was deadly. A greeter at a Wal-Mart in New York was trampled to death by shoppers eager to snatch up items on sale. Even as the man was dying under the feet of the stampede, one onlooker remarked, "Nobody was trying to help him. They were rushing into the store, rushing, rushing, rushing."[6]

Churches are not immune to the temptation to put money on the throne. We are often tempted to give our wealthier contributors more authority in church matters. Despite the clear warning of James against showing favoritism to the rich over the poor,[7] we bow before money's throne whenever we make decisions in order to appease fellow church members who are wealthy.

Some churches, by offering daycare for small children, unintentionally aid others in their unfettered pursuit of wealth. It would be terrific if churches were caring for the children of families struggling to put food on the table. Unfortunately, in most cases, the families that benefit from church day care have been deceived into thinking they need two incomes (just as they "need" a new car, a larger house, or more stuff to fill the house). Rather than modeling a lifestyle that challenges money's right to the throne, the church has often unwittingly aided and abetted others along in their idolatry.

INDEPENDENCE AND ISOLATION

Money can give us an unhealthy sense of independence or self-sufficiency. During my five years in Romania, I was not funded by any mission agency. The year before I moved overseas, I worked hard and saved money—funds that would cover much of my stay in Eastern Europe. Each summer, I would return home and work for a couple of months in order to save some money that would cover my expenses in Romania. I took pride in my independence!

Not long ago, I needed a few hundred dollars to cover some school costs. Someone in our church anonymously donated the needed funds. It went against my pride to accept the gift. I thought to myself, *I managed to support myself and my family for five years in Romania! I should be able to cover my own school costs!*

My pastor gently rebuked me: "Trevin, every single penny you receive comes from someone else's hand. Your paycheck has to be given to you, just like a donation has to be given to you. Just say, 'Thank you,' and receive God's provision." My attitude had been wrong. I had bought into the false idea that everything I owned, I had earned. But my pastor was right. I was succumbing to one of the subtle temptations of money—thinking that I was independent, when even my ability to earn money was given to me by God.

When we sacrifice relationships for money, show favoritism based on financial status, or display a false sense of independence, we become more and more isolated from other people. The Caesar of Money specializes in loneliness.

Popular singer/songwriter John Mayer described the isolation that comes from rampant materialism in his song "Something's Missing":

> I'm dizzy from the shopping malls,
> I searched for joy, but I bought it all . . .
> Something's missing and I don't know how to fix it,
> Something's missing and I don't know what it is . . .
> I wish there was an over-the-counter test for loneliness . . .
> How come everything I think I need always comes with batteries?[8]

Jesus also spoke to the isolation and loneliness that comes from greed and covetousness. In Luke 12, he tells a story about a rich man who closely resembles the people featured in the *Tennessean* article about storage units. The rich man has no place for his "stuff." And Jesus shows us how isolated this man has become:

> The land of a rich man produced plentifully, and he thought to himself, "What shall I do, for I have nowhere to store my crops?" And he said, "I will do this: I will tear down my barns and build larger ones, and there I will store all my grain and my goods. And I will say to my soul, Soul, you have ample goods laid up for many years; relax, eat, drink, be merry." But God said to him, "Fool! This night your soul is required of you, and the things you have prepared, whose will they be?" So is the one who lays up treasure for himself and is not rich toward God. (Luke 12:16–21)

It is significant that Jesus describes the rich man talking to himself about his surplus problem. In Middle Eastern culture, if a problem like this surfaced, a man would sit at the gate with other men and discuss possible solutions. He would talk to family, friends, or neighbors. This was the kind of decision that he would make with the consultation of the community, not by himself.[9] But Jesus shows us a man who is isolated. He never mentions anyone else. No family. No friends. No one. The man's surplus has brought loneliness.

People who become consumed with thoughts about their possessions tend to retreat further and further into their own world. Some people become so stingy with their dollars they are afraid to trust anyone.

Last century, Howard Hughes, one of the richest men in the world, demonstrated how money can bring loneliness. By the world's standards, Hughes had it all—wealth, power, sex, and success. But this man concluded his life holed up in a dark room, shut off from the world. Money is a terrific servant, but a terrible master.

The rich man in Jesus' story plots out his future. He uses the pronoun "I" or "my" more than ten times in these verses. "What shall *I* do, for *I* have nowhere to store *my* crops? *I* will do this: *I* will tear down *my* barns and build larger ones, and there *I* will store all *my* grain and *my* goods."

Whenever I read this story, I picture Gollum from the *Lord of the Rings* stroking the ring of power and saying over and over again, "It's *mine*—my precious." Gollum is consumed by his obsession with the ring. Likewise, when we take God's good gift of money and make it ultimate in our lives, we become idolaters. We are sacrificing to the Caesar of Money and adopting a materialistic mind-set that sees money as the ultimate goal of life and work.

SUBVERTING MONEY

Zacchaeus, a Bible character forever known in the children's song as "a wee little man," was a tax collector who ripped off his neighbors and pocketed his profit at their expense. An encounter with Jesus changed Zacchaeus forever. As Zacchaeus hosted Jesus in his home, he said, "Behold, Lord, the half of my goods I give to the poor. And if I have defrauded anyone of anything, I restore it fourfold." Jesus replied, "Today salvation has come to this house!"[10] Salvation works itself out in the renewal and restructuring of a person's entire life, including money and finances.

If we are living under the lordship of Jesus, our lives cannot stay the same. True repentance reaches into our checkbooks and makes changes, shuffling our priorities. True repentance cancels debts, transforms our vision, reforms our desires, modifies our dreams, and heals our hurt and the hurt of others. The apostle Paul commands us to put to death our covetous behavior, and he equates greed with idolatry.[11]

Christians are called to be generous, not greedy, because our wealth and our lives are a gift from God. There are three main ways in which we can subvert the Caesar of Money: by demonstrating to the world that all money comes from God; by embracing a mind-set that focuses on eternal investments instead of temporal trivialities; and by showing the world through our choices that people matter more than possessions.

Demonstrate to the World That All Money Comes from God's Hand

Once God saves us, our vision of wealth should be transformed. We should begin seeing ourselves as stewards, people who have been given the responsibility to handle God's money.

The earliest Christians believed that money was *from* God and *for* God. They did not look at money as something that belonged solely to them. Money needed to be shared. Acts 2 describes the way early Christians viewed their possessions:

> And all who believed were together and had all things in common. And they were selling their possessions and belongings and distributing the proceeds to all, as any had need. (Acts 2:44–45)

The example of the early church should cause us to rethink our entire view of work. In our society today, many of us no longer find value in the work we do as image-bearers of the Creator. Instead, we find meaning in the money we earn, not the work we do. Money buys material possessions that are supposed to give our lives meaning and fulfillment. It is no surprise, then, that many hold a forty-hour-a-week job simply to receive the paycheck. Many stay in a certain job to receive a promotion that will give them more benefits. Others work because they hope for a good bonus at the end of the year.

Earning Money in Order to Give

Speaking to the Ephesian elders, the apostle Paul quoted the words of Jesus: "It is more blessed to give than to receive."[12] Yes, we are blessed to receive a paycheck. God blesses our labor. He wants us to work at our jobs with all our hearts, as unto him. But the bigger blessing comes to those who give. And that leads us to rethink why we work forty hours a week anyway. We all work to gain. But do we work to *give*? Do our spending habits reflect the truth that our money comes from God?

The apostle Paul claims that the reason we should labor is so that we "may have something to share."[13] This cuts against both the conservative mind-set that sees everyone individually fending for themselves and the liberal mind-set that keeps entire groups of people dependent on government funds. Paul tells the nonworker to stop being a parasite in the community, and instead to get a job and start helping others. But he tells the diligent worker to keep on laboring, so that he can receive the blessing that comes from giving.

Too many of us think only of receiving. The bigger our paycheck, the better our house, the nicer our car, the more prestige we obtain in the eyes of others. Jesus' way is radically different: the bigger our paycheck, the more we can give away.

It is terrific to see local churches with a biblical vision of giving. I recently heard about a church plant that wanted to be missions-focused. The church gave 33 percent of its offerings directly to missions. As the congregation grew, members began mulling over the decision to purchase a building. The percentage they gave to missions would go down temporarily, but as the number of congregants continued to grow, the actual dollar amount of giving to missions would go up. Some in the church wanted to stay small and give a big percentage. Others wanted to grow and give a larger sum.

Regardless of who was right or wrong in the discussion of

that church's future vision, *both* sides were modeling a mind-set that is subversive of the world's view of money. Both saw missions and giving as vital. Both saw the church not as the final destination for money, but as the funnel for funds to flow out to others. Both were demonstrating a heartfelt commitment to "distribute the proceeds" wisely.

Giving Freely and Generously

The stories of Scripture demonstrate how the idolatry of covetousness can easily grip our hearts. Even many Old Testament heroes were motivated by greed or covetousness at times. But Jesus came to free us from the grip of money by offering his blood on the cross. By freely giving up his life, he set us free from the Caesar of Money. But more than that, his death frees us in order that we might give freely and generously to others.

When I first visited Romania as a fifteen-year-old, I met a variety of Romanian village and city pastors. One pastor had a son who was mentally and physically handicapped. The pastor's wife looked malnourished and worn. Nevertheless, this pastor and his wife hosted me and my father in their home, gave us opportunities to minister in village churches, and demonstrated a love for God's people.

My father felt the Spirit leading him to help cover the costs of the medical bills for their child. Having come to know this family, however, we realized that they would not accept our charity. I can still remember what my father did right before we left their apartment. When he knew no one could see him, he started stuffing Romanian currency in between the pillows on the couch, hiding some money on top of the refrigerator, and putting bills in the coat pockets of the family. The reckless abandon and glee with which he "threw away" that money made a profound impact on me. Money's power is renounced when we give it away freely.

Tithes and Offerings

One way we show that all we have belongs to God is by setting aside a portion of our income for the work of God in the local church. We give of our firstfruits, not our leftovers. The apostle Paul instructed the Corinthians in this way:

> Now concerning the collection for the saints: as I directed the churches of Galatia, so you also are to do. On the first day of every week, each of you is to put something aside and store it up, as he may prosper, so that there will be no collecting when I come. (1 Cor. 16:1–2)

As our income increases ("as we prosper") we should give away higher percentages of our income. Those who have been blessed with much are responsible for much.[14] Biblical giving is much more than giving away what we could afford to do without. C. S. Lewis wrote:

> I am afraid the only safe rule is to give more than we can spare. In other words, if our expenditure on comforts, luxuries, amusements, etc., is up to the standard common among those with the same income as our own, we are probably giving away too little. If our charities do not at all pinch or hamper us, I should say they are too small. There ought to be things we should like to do and cannot do because our charitable expenditure excludes them.[15]

Embrace a Mind-set That Focuses on Eternal Investments over Temporal Trivialities

Jack Benny was a comedian who performed on old-time radio and television. His running gag centered on his stinginess. In Benny's most popular routine, a robber would put a gun to his back and say, "Your money or your life." A long pause would follow. The audience would start laughing. After a few moments, the robber would say again, "Your money or your life!" Jack Benny would reply, "I'm thinking! I'm thinking!"

We laugh at Jack Benny's warped perspective (after all, what good is money without your life?), but part of the reason we laugh is because we are also tempted by this false perspective. We spend so much time thinking about our temporal happiness that we lose sight of the nature of eternity.

Imelda Marcos, the former first lady of the Philippines, was famous for her shoe collection. While her people languished in poverty, she had a closet filled with more than three-thousand pairs of shoes. She sometimes remarked about what a burden her shoe collection could be! Wealth often warps our perspective. Possessions too quickly crowd people out of our lives as we focus on the temporary over the eternal.

Jesus tells us to "lay up for yourselves treasures in heaven."[16] We should do something eternal with our money. It is shameful to waste it all on ourselves. We should invest money by pouring it into bettering someone's life, not just enhancing our own living.

An Eternal Perspective

One of my favorite prayers in the Bible, from the book of Proverbs, says:

> Give me neither poverty nor riches; feed me with the food that is needful for me, lest I be full and deny you and say "Who is the LORD?" or lest I be poor and steal and profane the name of my God. (Prov. 30:8–9)

This prayer helps us to avoid orienting our lives around money—either by how much or how little we have. After all, even a poor person can be consumed by possessions. It's not about how much we have or don't have; it's about our perspective. Are we focusing on the eternal? Or do we think of money in terms of the temporary trivialities it can buy?

The rich man in Jesus' story is called a "fool" because, despite all of his economic calculations, he did not consider his own mortality. Christians should not fall into this trap. It should be true of every one of us that if someone were to look over our bank statement, they would see evidence that we view wealth as a gift—a temporary gift to be used and given back to God.

We subvert the world's preoccupation with wealth-building by focusing on eternal investments that may not pay earthly dividends. Consider a man who has a well-paying job in a town where his family is happy and established. They are active in their church and community. He is offered a sizable promotion, as long as he agrees to move across the country. Taking into consideration his family's spiritual well-being, this man might decide to forego the extra money. Why? Because the Caesar of Money is not dictating to him what his decision should be; Jesus is.

Christian families subvert the world's view of money by rejecting the idea that all families should have dual incomes. The mother who sacrifices her career path in order to stay home and raise the children is acting in a deeply subversive manner. The family that lives on one income may get by with only one car, a smaller house, and fewer of the trappings of our materialist culture. But the eternal investment in the family is incalculable. I have never heard people on their deathbed weeping over lost time in the business world, the car they never had, or the dream house they never built. Usually, people weep over lost opportunities to invest in others.

When Christians subvert the Caesar of Money, other people take notice. Sociologist Lisa Keister has done research showing that conservative Protestants save less and accumulate fewer assets than other Americans, and she chalks up their lower wealth to their religious beliefs. Keister found that conservative Protestants believe that people are managers of God's money and that excess accumulation of wealth should be avoided. Furthermore, she discovered that these Christians have larger families at younger ages, and that fewer of the women work outside the home. "Some people have just decided that saving money in my own bank account isn't what they want," Keister told a reporter, also noting that conservative Protestants are the most generous contributors to churches and charities.[17]

As Christians, we should astound others with our generosity. We should be the biggest tippers at the restaurant, the biggest contributors to worthy causes, and the first to volunteer our time and money for the church. When we live subversively, we will attract attention, not only from sociologists, but also from our neighbors, family, and friends. Our lives should be a testament to the world that Jesus is king and money is not.

Show the World That People Matter More Than Possessions

Many who are reading this book may be in the midst of financial troubles and are struggling to pay the bills. I think back to my time in a Romanian village in a home with no indoor plumbing. I realize that this chapter might seem practical for only those who have been blessed with a surplus. But what about those who are barely making enough to get by? Many citizens of God's kingdom have very few possessions to give. Can poor Christians be subversive of the Caesar of Money?

Though the amount of money that low income families can contribute to worthy causes will be less than the amount the wealthy can give, all are commanded to contribute. When Jesus saw the poor woman giving her last penny into the temple treasury, he did not stop her, return her money, and then offer her charity. No! He accepted her gift and honored her sacrifice.[18] Christians who are poor actually have the opportunity to exceed the good works of rich Christians, because they contribute out of their poverty instead of their abundance.

Christians with few resources may never be able to give large sums of money. But even the poor can demonstrate to the world that people matter more than possessions. Many times in Romania, I witnessed villagers giving to those poorer and needier than themselves. I never saw Christians turn away those who asked for food. They gave them what they had, even if it meant they would eat less that night.

We must be careful not to set up an economic barrier between the rich and the poor, seeing a church as merely doing ministry *for* the poor. We ought to be breaking down economic barriers so that we can minister *alongside* the poor to other poor people. In Christ we are no longer rich or poor, slave or free. We are united, not by our economic standing, nor even by our ministry to the needy, but by our citizenship in the kingdom of God.

As I write this chapter, Americans are receiving economic stimulus checks. The government believes people will buy something impulsively, and that their purchases will jump-start our lagging economy. People have already begun asking friends what they plan on doing with the money from the stimulus checks. What better testimony could Christians give than to say: *We put some in the bank, we spent a little bit, and we gave much of it away.* Or, *We gave to a mission organization in Africa that is feeding the hungry and sharing the gospel.* Or, *We gave to a missionary in East Asia who is training new pastors.* What better way to show the world that people matter more than possessions than to forego our desire for a big-screen TV and invest in others' lives!

FOOLS FOR CHRIST

In Jesus' parable about the rich man who wanted to build bigger barns, he called the man "a fool." In the eyes of the world, the rich man was a successful entrepreneur and a terrific business-man. But by putting money on the throne, the rich man was foolish.

In the eyes of the world, Christians look foolish. When we subvert money by placing it under Jesus' feet, we shift our priorities. People scratch their heads and ask why we are spending or saving or giving in the way that we do. But I would rather be a fool in the eyes of the world than a fool in the eyes of Jesus.

The song "Only a Fool" by Geoff Moore and the Distance puts it well:

> Charlie was a fool.
> Did you hear what he went and did?
> He quit his job, threw it away,
> Gave his life to a bunch of kids . . .
>
> Show me the big in the small
> Show me the beauty in the call
> Show me the road that I should choose
> I'll take the job only a fool could do.[19]

SUBVERTING LEISURE
Making Jesus Lord of Our Free Time

IN THE LATE 1940s, George Orwell wrote a popular work of fiction entitled *1984*. Orwell's dystopian novel describes a future world in which an all-observing government ("Big Brother") bans books, suppresses original thought, and polices all activities. For several decades, as Communism was rising in the East, many in the West feared that Orwell's vision of a worldwide totalitarian regime might soon come to pass. But after Communism collapsed in Eastern Europe, the threat of such a regime diminished. Instead, the fictional world described in a different book, Aldous Huxley's *Brave New World* (released in 1932) has become more likely.

Huxley's vision of the future stands in stark contrast to Orwell's. In *Brave New World*, the danger is not that books would be banned, but that people would be so entertained they would have no use for reading them. The hedonistic society in Huxley's book thrives on promiscuous sexual behavior, government-sponsored drugs, environmental conditioning, and genetic manipulation. Whereas Orwell envisioned a world in which the government used technology to hold people captive against their will, Huxley described a world in which people would *love* the technology that held them captive.[1] Many aspects of *Brave New World* frighteningly resemble contemporary American culture. We live in a world of constant entertainment.

OUR ENTERTAINMENT-SATURATED SOCIETY

Human beings bear the image of a God who works and rests. In the first chapters of Genesis, we see God working to create the world and then resting from his labors.[2] The divine rhythm of work and rest was instituted in God's blessing of the Sabbath and in his command to the Israelites to keep the day holy.[3] According to Scripture, rest and leisure are gifts from God.

Although leisure is a good gift from God, it can easily take the place of God in our lives. When leisure becomes our reason for living, it stops being a friend and becomes a harsh taskmaster. We are robbed of the joy of working to the glory of God[4] whenever our labor becomes simply a means to an end—a vacation, a new technological gizmo, or more time off for sporting events. This insidious Caesar blinds our vision so that we no longer see the danger in spending exorbitant amounts of money and time on nonstop entertainment.

Television

I often wonder what people from an underdeveloped country (a place where homemade shrines to idols are still prevalent) might think if they could see the layout of the typical American living room. Might they ask, "What is that boxed idol in the center of the room that everything points to? Why do you spend so much time at your shrine to that box? What does it do for you?"

In a roundtable discussion with Silicon Valley investors, the CEO of TiVo (the digital television recorder), Michael Ramsay, spoke to the issue of "storage anxiety." Consumers get anxious because they record so many television programs on their TiVo that they are unable to find time to watch them all. Investor Roger McNamee piped up, saying, "We just want to have a ton of stuff on some storage thing somewhere so that when the urge hits us, we can be entertained!"[5]

Pastor John Piper writes:

> Television is one of the greatest life-wasters of the modern age. . . . The main problem with TV is not how much smut is available, though that is a problem. Just the ads are enough to sow fertile seeds of greed and lust, no matter what program you're watching. The greater problem is banality. A mind fed daily on TV diminishes. Your mind was made to know and love God. Its facility for this great calling is ruined by excessive TV. The content is so trivial and so shallow that the capacity of the mind to think worthy thoughts withers, and the capacity of the heart to feel deep emotions shrivels.[6]

Television saturates our lives with mindless entertainment, and then isolates us from other people. Before TV, families created their own entertainment, often gathering around the fireplace for stories or around the piano to sing some favorite songs. The front porch was a staple of American society, a place for neighbors to stop by and catch up on the latest news.

After the onset of television, front porches disappeared. The living room, once the "sitting room," morphed into the main hub of entertainment in the house. The fragmentation began. Families isolated themselves from their neighbors, choosing the banter of neighbors on TV sitcoms rather than real conversation with neighbors across the street.

At least in the early years of television, watching TV still remained a family event. Friends and family gathered together to watch the best comedies and variety shows. But now, as television variety has increased, so has the number of televisions in a home. Children have Nickelodeon at the foot of their beds; preteens have the Disney Channel; teenagers have MTV. Newspapers are now reporting that in many homes, different tastes in television programs have caused husbands and wives to stop watching TV together. He goes one way; she goes another. The fragmentation is now complete. There's something to appeal to everyone. From the entertainer's viewpoint, everyone wins! But in reality, everyone loses.

Busyness

My Romanian friends and family who visit the United States find it remarkable that Americans seem to have little time for friends and neighbors. We keep to ourselves. We devote our time to the Caesar of Leisure and entertainment. We sacrifice our free time to the television and the Internet. Filling our lives with perpetual entertainment has become easier than ever. One can now download movies to a cell phone or listen to virtually any type of music on a portable MP3 player.

The Caesar that would hold us captive to our free time even affects our children. Parents taxi children from one event to another, focusing all their leisure time on dance classes, organized soccer, Little League, or music lessons. Many times the children are as unhappy with their hurried lifestyle as the parents, and if given the choice, would simply want to go home. When we allow sports, recreation, and other leisure activities to dictate our schedules, we and our children suffer.

Video Games

In recent years, the Caesar of Leisure has become prominent in the proliferation of video games. For many families, the Xbox is in charge.

When I was attending seminary in Louisville, I spent my afternoons tutoring young elementary and middle-school students in failing Kentucky schools. The tutoring job provided me a unique opportunity to enter a family's home for a couple of hours twice a week and assess the family dynamic. Sadly, I realized that many of these children did not need a tutor; they needed a parent.

One sixth-grade boy was failing in school because he played video games eight hours every night. Yes, eight hours per night! The bookshelves in his room were full, not of books, but of game cartridges. It was no wonder that the boy was falling asleep in school and could barely read. Frustrated with his addiction to video games, the parents took his bedroom door off its hinges. I found it odd that they could take such a radical step to monitor their son's entertainment consumption, and yet never consider the simpler step of unplugging his personal TV and game system.

One of my other students also played video games for many hours every evening. But when I asked his father about the wisdom in playing Nintendo for so long, he replied, "Actually, *I'm* the one who's playing. He just watches."

Hollywood and the Church

The church has not always properly subverted leisure and entertainment. Pastors today can find a variety of Web sites that offer free clips from popular, current movies to spice up their sermons. Hollywood woke up to the potential to make money off evangelicals after the stunning success of *The Passion of the Christ*. Now, Hollywood markets anything even remotely "family friendly" to the church.

To top it off, Hollywood offers sermon ideas inspired from each film clip. Why not do a sermon series on revenge and show a *Spiderman 3* clip each week? How convenient that the marketers of *Spiderman 3* provided churches with film clips to coincide with the film's opening weekend! Instead of offering something of substance, we have chosen to offer the same kind of banality people can find anywhere else.

HOLY SUBVERSION

Most evangelicals watch the same movies as everyone else. We are the ones attending church on Sunday mornings and watching *Desperate Housewives* on Sunday nights. In our desire to receive Hollywood's approval and attention, we allow the movie-making industry to take up minutes of precious pulpit time on a Sunday morning to market their movies when pastors should be declaring, "Thus says the Lord . . . "

SUBVERTING LEISURE

Devotion to leisure did not appear with the onset of television, but has long been a struggle for Christians throughout history. In the Roman Empire, the rulers knew they could stay in power if they pacified the populace with enough food on the table and enough public entertainment. Juvenal, an ancient satirist, called the Roman policy "bread and circus."[7] If you keep bellies full of food and minds occupied with shows and games, you keep control. One of the ways the Caesars solidified their power was through mass entertainment.

The early Christians did not deny that sports and entertainment could have a legitimate place in a person's life. In his letters, the apostle Paul included athletic metaphors mentioning the value of bodily training[8] and the rules by which an athlete must play.[9] Paul spoke of himself as running the race of faith[10] and straining forward to "the prize of the upward call of God in Christ Jesus."[11]

However, Christians also saw how love for the arena and the theater could become idolatrous. As they witnessed the pagans' worship of sports and entertainment, Christians subverted leisure by standing against the decadence and wastefulness of the entertainment mind-set.[12]

The early Christians subverted leisure as they imitated Christ, the Son of God who lived according to his Father's timetable.

Jesus came not to be served and pampered with the luxuries of this world, but to fulfill his kingdom mission. He also instructed his followers to seek first the kingdom.[13] Christians recognized that a life of perpetual leisure competes with a life that is on mission for God.

The Christian's life is not grounded in leisure; it is grounded in the cross. If we have truly been set free from the bondage of sin and death, then we have been set free from the slavery of perpetual leisure that would have us live only for ourselves. We have been delivered from the desire for constant entertainment and the never-ending pursuit of our own pleasure. God has given us freedom from leisure, and he has also given us a task. We are called to proclaim the good news of God's kingdom. As the Father sent Jesus, so Jesus has sent us.[14]

Therefore, the way we spend our free time reveals what we believe about God. If we are imaging God rightly by following his instructions for resting and working, we will not allow leisure to take the throne of our lives. As we put leisure back in its proper place under the lordship of Jesus, we will make different choices when it comes to our leisure activities.

There are three main ways that we as Christians can subvert leisure and entertainment. First, we must think seriously about the choices we make regarding our free time. Next, we must purposefully structure our free time in a way that glorifies God. Finally, we must turn our focus away from the things that entertain us to the people that God has entrusted to us.

Thinking Seriously about Our Free Time

Free time is not a trivial matter. The activities we participate in during our moments of leisure shape our identity.

Thinking seriously about free time means we must resist the temptation to check our minds at the door when we are being entertained. Sometimes I hear fellow believers talking about how much they enjoyed a recent movie that carries a blatantly anti-Christian message. If I ever inquire about a movie's philosophy or teaching, I sometimes receive this reply: "Can't you just enjoy the movie? When I go to the theater, I don't want to think! I just want to take it in."

Such a mindless attitude towards entertainment is devastating for the Christian. If we are to love the Lord our God with all our heart, soul, and mind,[15] then we must avoid giving Hollywood maximum power to form us into the image of this world. The apostle Paul encourages us to have our minds renewed:

> I appeal to you therefore, brothers, by the mercies of God, to present your bodies as a living sacrifice, holy and acceptable to God, which is your spiritual worship. Do not be conformed to this world, but be transformed by the renewal of your mind, that by testing you may discern what is the will of God, what is good and acceptable and perfect. (Rom. 12:1–2)

Thinking seriously about our free time means we should carefully monitor the shows that our children watch, too. Television advertising tells our children, at the earliest ages, what they "need" to make them happy. Many of today's cartoons tell children that they need only listen to their heart and believe in themselves in order to succeed in life.

Recently, I sat down with my son to watch an old Disney videotape that had some cartoons from the 1960s. I was horrified to see that one of the cartoons featured Jiminy Cricket singing these words to a catchy melody:

You are a human animal.
You are a special kind of breed.

For you are the only animal who can think, who can reason,
    who can read!
The only human animal is you, you, you![16]

Right there in our living room, the television was telling my child he is an animal, and that the only aspect that separates him from animals is his ability to think and reason. What about the mentally handicapped child? What about the elderly woman who loses the ability to read? Are they nothing more than animals? A cute little cricket was making bold statements about humanity that contradict the biblical definition of human worth and dignity. We must be constantly on guard, always thinking seriously about the messages coming from the television.

Structuring Our Free Time to the Glory of God

The New Testament demonstrates a sense of urgency when speaking about the last days. The apostle Paul writes:

> Look carefully then how you walk, not as unwise but as wise, making the best use of the time, because the days are evil. Therefore do not be foolish, but understand what the will of the Lord is. (Eph. 5:15–17)

Paul tells us not to make *good* use of our time, but to make the *best* use of our time. His understanding of the present evil age leads him to strong exhortation regarding the way followers of Jesus must manage our time.

Our lives are so short. James reminds us that our life is little more than "a mist that appears for a little time and then vanishes."[17]

Why then do we fritter so much of our lives away in front of the television screen?

Why do we spend every evening playing or watching sports?

Why do we spend our weekends roaming the shopping malls, looking at more things we do not need?

Jesus tells us to seek first the kingdom of God and his righteousness. Seeking first the kingdom means we are *not* seeking after the same things as the pagan world around us: food, drink, and clothing.[18] We must take a good look at our lives.

Do we shop as often, and for the same things, as our non-Christian neighbors?

Do we covet all the newest fashions?

Are we as drawn to the latest technological gizmos as everyone else?

Too often, we give lip service to seeking first the kingdom, while our lives demonstrate pagan preoccupations.

Prioritizing Our Faith

Structuring our free time in a God-honoring way means we will prioritize our leisure activities so that it is clear that Jesus is on the throne of our lives. We will make time for daily Bible study and prayer. We will share meals around the table instead of in front of the tube. We will engage in family prayer and worship. And when our devotion to Jesus collides with the temptation to put something else on the throne, we will demonstrate to the world who is our king.

Sports

One way we can prioritize our activities is quite practical. Many organized sports leagues now play soccer or softball on Sundays, as though it were any other day. What should a Christian do in this situation?

Here's another example: While in high school, my brother played for an advanced soccer league that practiced every Wednesday night during the church's youth group hour. My brother was faced with a dilemma: should he sacrifice his potential soccer scholarship in order to attend church? Or should he sacrifice Jesus on the altar of his sports ambitions? I was proud of his choice to fellowship with the body of Christ, even if it meant he sacrificed playing time during the games. (Later, he was awarded a soccer scholarship to a Christian university!)

Too many Christians pay lip service to Jesus as king and yet demonstrate by their recreational choices that something else is on the throne. Ball is Ba'al. When parents replace Sunday morning worship with a Sunday morning ball game, they are communicating more to their children through that one action than many years' worth of words stressing the importance of church attendance.

Planning Quiet Moments

Another way that we can structure our free time in a way that is subversive of the Caesar of Leisure is by planning moments of contemplative solitude. The constant barrage of noise and entertainment today can effectively drown out the voice of God to us, so that even when we open the Scriptures, we are too distracted to hear what God has to say.

I confess that it is often difficult for me to fit regular times of quiet prayer and contemplation into my schedule. My responsibilities to family, church, and school keep me busy. But even though long periods of silence and prayer may be difficult for me during this stage of my life, it is still important that I seek out those quiet moments with God, even if they are just moments and not hours.

A spiritual discipline that helps keep my life centered on Christ is the practice of praying briefly three or four times a day at certain hours. The Old Testament saints prayed in this manner, as have many Christians throughout the centuries. Prayer books can help guide you through certain psalms and Scriptures during these quiet moments. Praying at fixed hours keeps my focus and attitude on the kingdom of God and helps me add a spiritual structure to a schedule that can too easily become controlled by entertainment (TV schedule), food (three meals a day), or work (clock in, clock out).

Francis Schaeffer writes:

> No one seems to want (and no one can find) a place of quiet—because, when you are quiet, you have to face reality. But many in the present generation dare not do this because on their own basis reality leads them to meaninglessness; so they fill their lives with entertainment, even if it is only noise. . . . The Christian is supposed to be very opposite: There is a place for proper entertainment, but we are not to be caught up in ceaseless motion which prevents us from ever being quiet. Rather we are to put everything second so we can be alive to the voice of God and allow it to speak to us and confront us.[19]

From the moment we awake to a noisy alarm clock, our lives are too often filled with constant noise throughout the day. What will this temptation be like for our children? If we do not teach them the value of quiet prayer and solitude, who will? Would it not be better to tuck our children into bed after a few moments of quiet prayer than to let them fall asleep under the glow of an impersonal television set at the foot of their bed?

Avoiding Time Wasters

Responsibly structuring our free time means we will avoid time wasters. Some Christians have decided to toss out the TV altogether, and they will tell you afterwards how wonderful it has been for their family. I applaud Christians who decide to take this radical step of cutting television out of their lives.

Some might not go so far as to throw out the TV, but certainly we should all consider "fasting" from television for a month or two, preferably before Christmas or Easter. Other Christians intentionally limit the amount of time they spend in front of the television.

Just recently, my wife and I decided to return the cable box to the cable company. We didn't watch enough TV to merit the monthly fee, and we were sickened by the filth coming over the airwaves, even on the so-called "Family Plan." When I called the cable company, the man on the telephone tried to haggle with me so I could get *more* channels for better prices. When he realized I was serious about cutting off the cable, he told me that I would receive a one-time penalty fee on my account. I was getting my hand slapped for downgrading? When I returned the cable box to the company, I noticed the clerk's eyes got big, and she asked, "What's wrong?" The more people I talked to, the more I realized that the simple act of cutting the cable cord was subversive of leisure. The company seemed surprised that we could survive without cable!

Intentionality

We still have a television in our home, but my wife and I practice "intentional TV watching." Every now and then, we will purchase a DVD of a classic television show we enjoy, and over time, we will watch the episodes together. Intentional TV watching does away with channel surfing, not to mention the countless advertisements.

Making intentional choices about how much time to spend on entertainment should also be applied to video games. I am deeply grateful to my parents for limiting my access to computer games when I was growing up. My brothers and sister and I read books, wrote stories, made music, recorded shows on tape, played in the backyard, and even made our own movies! I am thankful that my parents did not give in to our persistent pleas for the newest video game.

But my parents also showed wisdom by not legalistically condemning all electronic entertainment. On rainy days, they would pull the Nintendo down from the closet shelf, dust it off, and let us play our hearts out. We still had fun playing video games, but my parents were wise enough to put the Nintendo back up when the sun returned. Even today, I still enjoy playing video games occasionally. Sometimes, after I finish a difficult semester of schoolwork, I will bring home some games to play with my little boy. We have a great time for a couple of days, but then we put the games away and move on to other things.

Leisure in its rightful place is terrific. Enjoying good, wholesome entertainment can be glorifying to God. But we must not underestimate the power of video games or television to affect how we view the world. Entertainment can and should be enjoyed, but it must never dominate our lives. Christians subvert leisure by limiting the time we spend on these activities. We structure our time in such a way that it is obvious to the world that we have different priorities.

Focusing Our Leisure Time on *People* Instead of Things

Some of my fondest memories of Romania are the long walks down the streets of the city, talking and laughing and enjoying friendships. My friends and I could have easily taken a tram or a taxi in order to arrive at our destination faster. But what would have been the purpose in hurrying? We had no TV to watch, no video games to play, nothing that had to be done in the next five minutes. So why *not* walk? Why *not* enjoy the fresh spring air? Why *not* talk on the way there?

When our free time revolves around constant entertainment, as is often the case in America, we miss out on what is best. We are enslaved to the fun of a fleeting moment, while missing out on relationships that could last a lifetime. The absence of constant entertainment is one reason many of my Romanian friendships seemed so much deeper than my American friendships. The Romanian friendships were built on quality time, good conversation, and honesty, whereas most of my American friendships were built on activities, hopping from one fun activity to the next, with very little time for quality conversation.

God has created us for more than shallow friendships that boil down to activities and entertainment that rob us of our time together. He desires us to have strong, healthy relationships with others. That will not happen unless we are spending time with people, not things.

Churches also must focus on people instead of entertainment. Some churches have chosen to wade in shallow waters, replacing the Word of God with a bombardment of fast-moving images on a big screen. Likewise, our church calendars are filled with so many programs that we hurry from one church activity to another: *game night, choir practice, youth activities, dramas, movie night, softball games, etc.* Of course, these activities can be good times of fellowship. But they can also sap us of our energy for true kingdom work and deceive us into thinking our busy calendar represents spiritual vitality.

IS IT WORTHY?

One evening in Romania, I went on a walk through the city. As I arrived back on the university campus, the sun was setting. I noticed a girl who had plopped down in the middle of the sidewalk, her eyes focused on the beautiful sunset. She looked at me and said, "It's worthy of stopping."

We declare something to be worthy by giving it our time and attention. Sports, movies, television, video games, shopping—all of these activities may be worthy of a place in our lives. But in a world in which people are bowing down to the Caesar of Leisure, spending so much time and energy in recreation and entertainment, Christians should intentionally seek to undermine the high status given to leisure by showing people that Jesus is more worthy.

For some, it will mean cutting out certain forms of entertainment completely. For others, it will mean sacrificing Sunday ballgames for Sunday worship. Our friends who are devoted to leisure might think we are crazy for cutting the cable cord, stopping our shopping sprees, praying at fixed hours, or missing some sporting events. Ironically, it is only when we put leisure back in its proper place under the lordship of Christ that we restore true sanity (the Apostle Peter calls it "sobermindedness"[20]) to our lives.

What we do with our free time shows who is king of our lives.

SUBVERTING SEX

Celebrating Marriage

DURING A RECENT hospital visit, my wife and I witnessed what has been dubbed "the vast wasteland" of daytime television. We caught part of an episode of *Judge Judy*, in which a young man was suing a young woman for cheating him out of $600. Apparently, he had moved into her apartment and was having sex with her regularly. Shortly after he paid her rent for the month, the girl dumped him. Furious and determined to get his money back, the young man took her to court.

What most surprised Judge Judy about this case was the nonchalant attitude that both individuals displayed towards sex. In her written statement, the young woman claimed that their relationship was nothing serious and that they were not dating—and yet they were sleeping together! "We were friends with benefits," the woman stated. Here were two adults living together, sleeping together, and yet claiming to not be in any sort of "romantic" relationship whatsoever. Judge Judy was right to be puzzled. Clearly something is wrong.

THE GOOD GIFT OF SEX

Human sexuality is one of God's good gifts to us. God has created us as sexual beings, and he intends for us to engage in sexual relations in the way he has prescribed.

Throughout church history, some Christians have downplayed the sacredness of sexuality. Informed and influenced by an unhealthy Greek asceticism, some early church fathers believed that all (or most) sexual activity was inherently sinful. By the time of the Reformation, the Roman Catholic Church had decided that there were 183 holy days in a year in which sexual activity was forbidden! The Reformers began to restore and reclaim the goodness of sexuality by celebrating it within the covenant of marriage.

It is not surprising that the holiness and sacredness of sexuality between husband and wife would be rediscovered by those who waved the flag of *sola Scriptura* ("Scripture alone" as the ultimate authority), since one can hardly begin reading the Bible without finding God's intention for sexual union. The very first commandment that God gives to humanity is to "be fruitful and multiply."[1] In other words, "Go make babies!" Within the first few pages of Genesis, we see the "one-flesh union" between man and woman in the covenant of marriage[2]—a union designed for the reproduction of humanity and the pleasure of God's people.

The Scriptures cherish the goodness of sexuality within the bounds of the marriage covenant. The sensual imagery of Song of Solomon is a case in point:

> Let him kiss me with the kisses of his mouth! For your love is better than wine; your anointing oils are fragrant. . . . Behold, you are beautiful, my love, behold, you are beautiful! You eyes are doves behind your veil. . . . How beautiful is your love, my sister, my bride! How much better is your love than wine, and the fragrance of your oils than any spice! Your lips drip nectar, my bride; honey and milk are under your tongue. . . . A garden locked is my sister, my bride, a spring locked, a fountain sealed. . . . My beloved has gone down to his garden to the beds of spices, to graze in the gardens and to gather lilies. (Song 1:2–3; 4:1, 10–12; 6:2)

Sex is indeed a good gift from God, a gift to be cherished in its rightful place. The Bible clearly and unapologetically confines sexual intimacy to the covenant of marriage between a man and a woman. It is only within this covenantal bond that sexuality can be experienced in its fullness, for it is only within marriage that sex glorifies God.

Lauren Winner rightfully points out the necessity of keeping sex and marriage tied together:

> When it comes to sex, one cannot leave out marriage. The *no* to sex outside marriage seems arbitrary and cruel apart from the Creator's *yes* to sex within marriage. Indeed, one can say that in Christianity's vocabulary the only real sex is the sex that happens in a marriage; the faux sex that goes on outside is not really sex at all. The physical commitment together that happens between two people who are not married is only a distorted imitation of sex, as Walt Disney's Wilderness Lodge Resort is only a simulation of real wilderness. The danger is that when we spend too much time in the simulations, we lose the capacity to distinguish between the ersatz and the real.[3]

THE CAESAR OF SEX

What happens when we take a good gift from God and make it ultimate in our lives? We worship the gift instead of the Giver, and the gift becomes our master.

Sex is one of the great Caesars of our day that holds people in its grip. The sexual revolution of the 1960s planted the seeds that have now become a harvest of heartbreak. Marriages are collapsing under the weight of sexual rebellion—whether in the forms of pornography or adultery. Marriage as an institution is crumbling under the weight of a divorce culture that no longer has the moral authority to clearly define marriage as a union between a man and a woman. What was once seen as "liberation" from traditional mores has now become a different type of slavery.

When we take God's good gifts and place them on the throne of our lives, we dehumanize ourselves and cheapen the gift of God. Even our talk about sex betrays our cheapened understanding and appreciation of this good gift from God. "Scoring," "hitting," and "shacking up" are casual ways of speaking of activity that, when properly defined, should actually be pointing us to God. The casual and nonchalant way we speak of sex shows how little we truly appreciate it. The Caesar of Sex continues to hold out the forbidden fruit of passion before our eyes, promising pleasure, but ultimately delivering despair, addiction, and heartbreak.

Perhaps our society's never-ending quest for the Caesar of Sex is actually an attempt to quench our thirst for transcendence with something or someone other than God. In a rationalistic, modern-day society where many of the leading intellectuals believe they can explain all human happenings scientifically, perhaps sex remains one of the last places of refuge for those seeking something that transcends the world of space, time, and matter—something that cannot quite be summed up in a scientific treatise. And yet our culture's obsession with sex may actually be a sign—not that we enjoy sex too much, but that we enjoy *true sex* too little.

SUBVERTING SEX

Throughout the Old Testament, the prophets connect sexual promiscuity with spiritual idolatry, and vice versa. This connection between spiritual idolatry and sexual promiscuity should remind us that sexuality is not some random issue unattached to our religious faith. Sexuality is a spiritual issue.

The New Testament era in which the church was born was not unlike our own. Some modern-day scholars would have us think of the Bible as an antiquated, outdated book whose authors could not possibly have been familiar with homosexuality, pedophilia, and other behaviors. But a brief look at the history of Roman culture dispels the notion that the early church was unfamiliar with aberrant forms of sexual behavior. In the Roman world, immorality was prevalent. Adultery was commonplace. Fornication was expected. Homosexuality was rampant and widely accepted among the populace.

The New Testament authors spoke out about homosexuality, fornication, and adultery, not because they did *not* know as much as we do about these sins, but because they *did*. In fact, the Bible affirms that some of the earliest converts to Christianity had turned from sexual sinfulness. The apostle Paul writes:

> Do you not know that the unrighteous will not inherit the kingdom of God? Do not be deceived: neither the sexually immoral, nor idolaters, nor adulterers, nor men who practice homosexuality, nor thieves, nor the greedy, nor drunkards, nor revilers, nor swindlers will inherit the kingdom of God. And such were some of you. But you were washed, you were sanctified, you were justified in the name of the Lord Jesus Christ and by the Spirit of our God. (1 Cor. 6:9–11)

The apostle Paul clearly forbids sexual immorality as an action that does not belong in the kingdom of God. Confessing Jesus as Lord is an action that demotes all rivals to his throne. Any sexual activity outside of the marriage covenant is in opposition to the kingdom inaugurated by Jesus Christ.

Yet, at the same time, Paul can say "such were some of you" at the end of his long list of sinful behaviors. In other words, within the redeemed church of Corinth were former thieves, idolaters, swindlers, and homosexuals. Paul does not lessen the grave nature of sexual sin, and neither does he lessen the magnitude of God's forgiveness for those who repent and trust in Jesus Christ.

The early Christians set an example of sexual behavior in the permissive atmosphere of the pagan world. Taking seriously the truth of their identity in Christ, the early Christians sought to live in a manner worthy of the kingdom of God, and in so doing, they exposed the idolatrous sexual activity of their surrounding culture.

If we are to show the world that Jesus is Lord and sex is not, then we must seek ways to subvert our culture's casual view of sex by demonstrating different practices that spring forth out of a biblical worldview. In our culture today, Christians who seek to live according to the Bible's picture of sexuality may appear strange or old-fashioned to others. But it is precisely our sexual peculiarity that offers the best picture of God's intention for true sexual fulfillment within the covenant of marriage.

We can subvert the Caesar of Sex by committing to the biblical virtue of chastity, celebrating sex within the covenant of marriage, refusing to separate sex from procreation, and by putting up proper boundaries around sexual temptation.

Committing to Chastity, Not Just Abstinence

In order to combat the toxic effects of the sexual revolution, many Christians have begun promoting abstinence in church youth groups and throughout the public school system. Abstinence curriculum tends to focus its efforts on scaring young people out of having sex. By showing the effects of sexually transmitted diseases, the teachers seek to demonstrate the weighty consequences of engaging in sex outside of marriage.

Abstinence education may be effective for the public school

system, but churches should not preach abstinence alone. After all, telling our young people that they should not have sex because of all the bad things that could happen to them actually perpetuates a self-centered view of sexuality. The teenagers who engage in sexual activity are having sex in order to please *themselves*. The teenagers who do not engage in sexual activity are not having sex in order to protect *themselves*. But the common root in both of these mind-sets is self-centeredness.

Furthermore, statistics are now showing that abstinence education often leads to a redefinition of sexuality and a loose definition of virginity. In 2003, researchers at Northern Kentucky University showed that 61 percent of students who signed sexual abstinence commitment cards broke their pledges. Of the remaining 39 percent of teenagers who kept their pledges, 55 percent admitted to engaging in oral sex. These statistics seem to indicate that a large number of young people do not consider oral sex to be sex. The definitions of what constitutes "sexual activity" are changing, which is why Christians must begin promoting chastity and not merely abstinence.

Promoting Purity

What is the difference between chastity and abstinence? Abstinence focuses on refraining from sexual intercourse, whereas chastity takes a more positive stance that affirms the cultivation of a purity that is pleasing to God. More than just a rule ("don't have sex before you're married"), chastity is a discipline. It is every bit as concerned with living purely as it is with refraining from sexual activity. The apostle Paul links sexual immorality and impurity together:

> Sexual immorality and all impurity or covetousness must not even be named among you, as is proper among saints. (Eph. 5:3)

Notice that the citizens of God's kingdom must live in accord with their identity as "saints." Sexual immorality, impurity, and covetousness should not even be named among us. Paul would not have us merely refrain from sexual immorality. He would have us cultivate lives of such devotion and purity that the slightest accusation of sexual impropriety could never stick.

Modesty

Chastity includes modesty. How we dress matters. Studies show that people who dress up on the day of an exam tend to score higher marks than those who dress sloppily. How we dress affects our behavior.

Women who dress provocatively should not be surprised at the attention they receive and the kind of men they attract. Sadly, the fashions on display in church on Sunday mornings or at Wednesday night youth services too often mirror the fashions of the world. Christians should be constantly modeling modesty in the way we dress and in the way we act.

Changing Our Questions

When chastity is properly cultivated, our questions should change. Instead of asking what constitutes "sexual behavior" or whether certain clothes pass the muster of "modesty," Christians should ask, "Is this holy? Is this pure? Will this cause someone to stumble? Is this glorifying to God?" Biblical chastity changes the questions and turns the negative prohibitions of abstinence into positive exhortations of purity.

Chastity is a spiritual discipline that we practice. We must not underestimate the sexual impulses of teenagers growing up in an increasingly sexually charged culture. Churches must begin to prepare young teenagers for the responsibilities of marriage while resisting the culture's infatuation with casual dating. The role of the church is invaluable in promoting chastity. Without the church walking alongside teenagers and singles who are actively seeking purity in thought and deed, we are bound for failure. We must hold one another accountable.

Celebrating Sex within the Marriage Covenant

If chastity is the rule for single people, then celebration is the command for married people. Sex must be properly celebrated within the proper biblical boundaries: marriage. C. S. Lewis writes:

> The Christian attitude does not mean that there is anything wrong with sexual pleasure, any more than about the pleasure of eating. It means that you must not isolate that pleasure and try to get it by itself, any more than you ought to try to get the pleasures of taste without swallowing and digesting, by chewing things and spitting them out again.[4]

Sex outside of marriage is an attempt to isolate sexual pleasure apart from its intended function. As Christians, we can subvert the Caesar of Sex, not by denying its goodness or downplaying its importance, but by celebrating it within its proper place: the marriage covenant. The writer of Hebrews says:

> Let marriage be held in honor among all, and let the marriage bed be undefiled, for God will judge the sexually immoral and adulterous. (Heb. 13:4)

The writer of Hebrews advocates a view of sexuality that is subversive of the world's mind-set in two ways. First, he believes marriage should be honored. It is doubtful that the writer of Hebrews was thinking of the institution of marriage (although we should, no doubt, honor marriage as a social institution as well). Instead, the author is most likely encouraging his readers to honor the marriages of the people in their congregations.

In a day and age where commitment to marriage has been diminished, surely we would do well to publicly recognize and honor the people in our congregations who have been married for decades. What would it look like if our churches were regularly celebrating marriage anniversaries together, honoring marriage publicly before an unbelieving world?

Second, the author of Hebrews is subversive in how he links together sex and marriage, moving seamlessly from speaking about marriage to speaking about the marriage bed. People today believe that sex can be divorced from marriage and that sexual behavior is no one else's business. If two adults consent to have sex, then no one (much less the church) should be allowed to challenge them.

But Scripture does not see sex in such an individualistic way. Since sex flows from the marriage covenant, and the marriage covenant is inherently communal (forming the foundation of the family as the bedrock of society), sex is necessarily everybody's business.

Once sex is seen in its proper place (tied to marriage), then our sexuality is connected to our marriages.

Our marriages form the foundation of our individual households.

Our households are under the umbrella of extended family.

Our extended families inhabit neighborhoods.

Neighborhoods form communities.

Communities form countries.

Sex is indeed everyone's business because it is communally linked to the marriage covenant, which is in its essence a *union* of two becoming one.[5]

A Covenant, Not Just a Contract

A biblical view of marriage will also celebrate the picture of the gospel that marriage is intended to put on display. Marriage has cosmic implications because it is a picture of God's covenant love for us in Christ.[6] When we minimize the sacredness of the gospel picture of marriage, we begin to treat marriage as a contract.

The main argument today in favor of same-sex marriage in the United States deals with the contractual rights and legal benefits that a civil marriage provides. Only in a society where the sacredness of marriage has already been devalued could we arrive at the stage where we speak of marriage only in contractual terms. *Who gets what? How can I sign this away? Who's in charge?*

As Christians, we subvert the Caesar of Sex by tying sexuality to marriage and by insisting that marriage is not a contract, but a covenant before God. Seeing marriage as purely contractual undermines marriage. That is why countries that long ago legalized same-sex unions have witnessed a dramatic reduction in the number of people getting married. Once sex is divorced from marriage and once marriage is no longer seen as sacred, the only people who continue the tradition of celebrating the marriage covenant are religious people who see a remnant of sacredness in the institution.

The prevailing view of marriage and sex in our society today actually makes it easier for Christians to subvert the Caesar of Sex. As we witness the devaluation of marriage and the abandoning of biblical sexuality, ordinary actions like saving sex for marriage, celebrating biblical marriage, and remaining faithful to our wedding vows become unusual. Christians stand out in a world of people who are settling for a sad series of "live-in" relationships.

The arrival of same-sex marriage in the United States is

indeed detrimental to American society, but this new development provides the church with a unique opportunity to counter the culture with a robust biblical worldview, through "ordinary" acts: practicing chastity, remaining faithful to our spouses, cherishing our marriage covenants, and recommitting to fidelity. It is in our "ordinary" acts that Jesus appears extraordinary to the world around us.

Refusing to Separate Sex from Procreation

A third way that we subvert the Caesar of Sex is by refusing to separate sex within marriage from the possibility of procreation. We must think biblically about children and resist the cultural urge to see sexuality as unattached to reproduction.

In the West, many couples are deciding to never have children. After all, children represent an imposition into one's daily life. Such a mind-set is inherently anti-biblical. The Scriptures see children as a blessing from the Lord.[7]

In Genesis 1:28 God commands Adam and Eve to "be fruitful and multiply." Notice that he does not say, "Go have sex." The commandment is for Adam and Eve to "go have sex *and children*." God repeats his command to Noah: "Fill the earth. Teem on the earth and multiply in it."[8] In Scripture, sex and reproduction go hand in hand.

When people choose to be deliberately childless over an extended period of time, they are rebelling against the Scriptural intention for sex. God does not intend that the marriage bed be inward-focused, but outward-focused, which means that marriages should be open to having children.

Once we expose the wrongheaded, individualistic view of sex in our culture today, we can put forth a better, more biblical picture—one that cherishes children as part of God's design for sex. Not every sexual act must end in reproduction, and planning responsibly for a family might include temporary use of birth control. (After all, mutual pleasure is one of the purposes of sex.) But Christian couples should display an attitude of openness to having children, a willingness to hold sex and procreation together.

While our friends and neighbors are choosing bigger homes, nicer cars, a second income, or a vacation in Europe, we should be having children. Yes, if we are having more children than everyone else, we might be seen as strange. Yes, if we decide that it would be better to have a child and postpone our dream house, others might scratch their heads. Yes, if Christians who are unable to have children of their own (or even those who are able!) choose instead to adopt, others might discourage them.

But it is precisely in our peculiar notions of keeping sex and reproduction tied together that we subvert the Caesar of Sex. We undermine the false notion that sexual activity is only about pleasure without the responsibilities of parenthood.

Putting up Proper Boundaries around Sexual Temptation

One final way that we can subvert the Caesar of Sex is by putting up boundaries that will keep us from sexual temptation. In the Sermon on the Mount, Jesus takes the Old Testament law forbidding sinful actions and intensifies that law until it includes sinful thoughts as well:

> You have heard that it was said, 'You shall not commit adultery.' But I say to you that everyone who looks at a woman with lustful intent has already committed adultery with her in his heart. If your right eye causes you to sin, tear it out and throw it away. For it is better that you lose one of your members than that your whole body be thrown into hell. And if your right hand causes you to sin, cut it off and throw it away. For it is better that you lose one

of your members than that your whole body go into hell.
(Matt. 5:27–30)

The radical nature of Jesus' command indicates the seriousness with which we are to guard against sexual sin. Cut off your hand. Gouge out your eye. If you are being led astray, do something drastic about it! Some well-intentioned Christians have taken this command literally, but Jesus is not promoting self-mutilation. He is using hyperbole in order to get the point across that we should do whatever it takes to cut off the lines to temptation. Do whatever it takes to live!

Aron Ralston was a 27-year-old mountain climber, hiking in an area where fewer than 100 people hike every year. Stopping to rest along the way, he somehow managed to get his arm pinned underneath an 800-pound boulder. Aron remained in the same place for five days, drinking the little water he had in his backpack and eating the last of his snacks.

On the fifth day, with rescuers still not able to find him, Aron took matters into his own hands. He used his T-shirt as a tourniquet and then used his pocketknife to saw off his own arm. The operation took an hour. After he cut his arm off, he was able to run down the mountainside to get help and medical attention. He survived only because he realized that unless he sacrificed what was holding him down, he would die.[9]

The urgency that Aron Ralston demonstrated in cutting off his arm is the kind of urgency we should demonstrate in our battle with lust. It may mean we cut off the Internet completely. It may mean we unplug the television. It will certainly mean that we stay away from places where we know we are likely to be tempted. Our eyes must be closed to temptation and wide open to the ways in which our culture would influence our view of sexuality.

Men must take drastic measures in order to protect themselves from Internet pornography. The stakes are too high. Internet pornography is instant, accessible, and anonymous. Without a monitoring program, even the most resolute of men may fall. Pornography keeps men from enjoying the fulfillment of true sexual union with their wives, offering instead a propped-up parody that robs them of the joyful expectations of fulfillment in marriage.

Women must beware of sexual seduction that comes through romance novels, soap operas, and television shows like *The Bachelor*. These materials serve the same function for women as pornography does for men. They are fantasy. They are foolish. They play to the lustful desires of the woman. In the same way that a wife feels she cannot compete for her husband's affection when he is accustomed to viewing pornography, neither can a husband compete with the fantasy novel's description of a strong, robust, attentive man sweeping a woman into his arms.

Christians must be conscious of the ways in which society is shaping our view of sexuality. We are subversive of the world's preoccupation with sex when we shun places of temptation and engage in acts of service. Sexual temptation and gratification will be naturally inward-focused unless we purposefully direct sex within marriage towards its cosmic goal: to picture the love of a God who is faithful to his covenant.

THE SELF-GIVING LOVE OF GOD

Standing against the tide of sexual permissiveness is not easy for Christians today. It is difficult to practice chastity in a culture that is increasingly pornographic. It is difficult to sustain healthy marriages in a divorce culture. It is difficult to cherish children in a society that sees them as a burden. It is difficult to win the war against lust when we are constantly bombarded with sexual temptation.

We are all sexual sinners. Our first response must be to throw ourselves upon the mercy of the God who has loved us and given himself for us. Jesus did not come to save us because of what we might do for him. He loved us with a selfless love, a self-giving love, a sacrificial love. He sacrificed himself so *we* could benefit from *him*.

Perhaps that is the most subversive message of all. In a day when the world sees immediate self-gratification as the ultimate end of so many things, including sex, we put before the world a startling picture of Jesus Christ sacrificing himself for us, paying the price for our sexual sin, and liberating us from the grip of this powerful Caesar.

SUBVERTING POWER

Finding Our Place as Servants

DURING MY SECOND YEAR of mission work in Romania, I was given the opportunity to serve one Sunday a month in a tiny village church close to the Hungarian border. As the months passed, it seemed the village became more desolate. The people were aging. Their children and grandchildren had moved to the cities. Whenever we walked down the main street, we passed rows of abandoned houses and saw brush overgrowing the courtyards.

The local Baptist church was merely a remnant of ten or so elderly members who, despite the decline of their village, were filled with hope. They loved the Lord, faithfully attended services, and consistently shared the gospel with their neighbors. They had been praying for a pastor, so they received great encouragement from our willingness to visit their church and minister to them once a month.

One day I was talking with a Romanian man who had just returned to the country, fresh out of seminary in the United States. He told me of his ongoing search for a church in which to serve. I informed him of the little village church that had long been praying for a pastor. His reply came swiftly: "I want a *city* church. I don't want to fool with the villages. City churches have a future. What can I do with a handful of people? I want a church I can grow."

HOLY SUBVERSION

The next time I ministered in the small village church, I could not help but wonder if maybe the seminary graduate was right. A pastor who would take such an insignificant church would be giving up any possibility of gaining power or influence within the Baptist Union. How foolish for a pastor with a seminary education to take a church with "no future"!

But as I listened to the joyful voices of the church members, believers remaining faithful even as their way of life crumbled around them, I came to see the power of God's kingdom in a unique way. The presence of the Lord seemed palpable in that little village church in the middle of nowhere. Somehow, serving in the place of powerlessness stirred up within me a powerful sense of hope and joy. I then felt sorry for my pastor friend. He was missing out on such a blessing!

POWER FROM ON HIGH

Power is a gift from God. After he created the world, God invested Adam and Eve with the authority to be rulers over creation. The first humans were given the responsibility of creating culture, subduing the earth, and cultivating a new life.[1] As a sign of his reign over creation, Adam went about naming the animals. And yet, God himself named Adam, which means that all human authority is ultimately delegated to us by God.[2] Whenever we rule wisely, we are reflecting the power of our good God and King.

Sin's corruption of power has caused many people today to harbor suspicions against institutional authority. Anyone who claims to know the truth about the world is suspected of being hungry for power, twisting the truth in order to rise above others. Many in the church eschew authoritativeness in church government or teaching. Some pastors shy away from the idea of "preaching" and choose instead to "give talks" or "facilitate discussion."

Although our culture demonstrates an aversion to power, we must not overlook the fact that God ordains structures of authority in our world. He expects humans to exercise their rightful authority, so long as that authority is exercised within the proper boundaries.

Take Moses, for example. God invested Moses with authority. In fact, he saw to it that Moses' dissenters were swallowed up by the earth![3] But when Moses overstepped his proper bounds of authority, God refused to let him enter the Promised Land.[4] With God-ordained authority comes much responsibility.

In matters of government, wise leaders seek accountability from their constituents. Within the framework of the United States Constitution is a system of checks and balances intended to keep one branch of the government from having too much power.

In New Testament times, Christians were encouraged to honor the emperor. Even though Christians were being persecuted by the Roman government, the apostle Paul indicated that Caesar has legitimate power, and yet he subversively undercut Caesar's claim to ultimate power by placing the Roman emperor under the authority of God.[5] Christians did not pray *to* the emperor, thus giving him honor and authority that was not his. They did, however, pray *for* the emperor[6] and, as a result, they recognized his lawful authority while going above him to God—the Sovereign One.

THE CAESAR OF POWER

The sin that plunged humanity into darkness was the coveting of power. Adam and Eve were unsatisfied with the authority that God had given them to exert. Ruling over the world as God's representatives was not enough. Satan deceived them, and the primeval couple wanted to "be like God."[7] They saw equality with God as something to grasp for, so they sinned.

Power is a seductive Caesar. Despite our postmodern aversion to institutional authority, we still crave positions of power. We can easily be controlled by the desire to either obtain or maintain whatever power we might have. During the process of grasping for or holding onto power, personal relationships are destroyed. As we demand more and more control, we trust others less and less. Trusting in oneself is the antithesis of putting proper trust in God.

Often our desire for power is evident in commonplace circumstances. In our marriages, we often lie in order to force our spouse to accommodate our desires. In social settings, we meet with friends or acquaintances for a meal and seek out the best seats or intentionally avoid socially awkward people. In church, we point to our financial resources, business prowess, or longstanding influence in order to sway people to our point of view.

When King Saul became corrupted by the Caesar of Power, he began pursuing David, the shepherd boy, in order to kill him—even though David was a popular warrior and the best friend of Saul's son.[8] King Saul wanted one of his most promising followers dead because he was too afraid to share power. Ironically, his devotion to power made him a weak and ineffective leader, intimidated by anyone who showed signs of promise.

But what if we want power in order to use it for good? In *The Lord of the Rings,* Gandalf the Grey is tempted by the power of the Ring because he considers all of the good he could accomplish. The Caesar of Power is most seductive when it appeals to our good instincts. Our initial desire for power could be well intentioned, but if we do not take great care in resisting power's insidious grip, we could still find ourselves at the feet of this Caesar. The scary fact is, we may never even realize it!

SUBVERTING POWER

The early Christians realized that power could be a corrosive influence. In order to subvert the Caesar of Power, they intentionally devoted themselves to imitating Jesus, the One who best exemplified humility in his willingness to sacrifice himself for our salvation. Whereas Adam saw equality with God as something to be grasped, Jesus saw the opposite. The apostle Paul writes:

> Have this mind among yourselves, which is yours in Christ Jesus, who, though he was in the form of God, did not count equality with God a thing to be grasped, but made himself nothing, taking the form of a servant, being born in the likeness of men. And being found in human form, he humbled himself by becoming obedient to the point of death, even death on a cross. Therefore God has highly exalted him and bestowed on him the name that is above every name, so that at the name of Jesus every knee should bow, in heaven and on earth and under the earth, and every tongue confess that Jesus Christ is Lord, to the glory of God the Father. (Phil. 2:5–11)

In our democratic society, it is easy to miss the implications of proclaiming someone as lord. The biblical picture is of a master who owns and has the right to command slaves. Our Bible translations today usually soften the idea of "slave" by rendering the Greek word as "servant" or "bondservant." But the New Testament does not describe the Christian as an employee or taxpayer with certain rights, but as slaves who owe everything to Jesus, the Master. We are slaves who have been transferred from the kingdom of darkness to the kingdom of light. We are people who owe faithful obedience to our King.

Even Paul, who had the authority of an apostle, refers to

himself as the slave of Jesus Christ.[9] Those who would seek to be leaders in the church would do well to remember that leadership begins with submission. Paul began several of his letters not by triumphantly proclaiming all the reasons why he had authority, but by modeling a cruciform life that resembled the life of Christ.

How can churches today learn to subvert the Caesar of Power without abandoning proper positions of authority? How do we celebrate power and authority within its proper place and yet keep this Caesar from taking the throne of our lives? First, we must rediscover the biblical truth that true strength is often found in what the world perceives as weakness. Next, we should begin sharing power, consciously rejecting the temptation to concentrate all power and authority in one place. Finally, we must actively seek to use power as a way to serve others.

Discovering True Strength in Weakness

In 1999, Governor Jesse Ventura famously claimed, "Organized religion is a sham and crutch for weak-minded people who need strength in numbers." Media mogul Ted Turner piped in with his own analysis of the church, saying that "Christianity is a religion for losers."

As Christians, we are tempted to react strongly against this kind of vitriolic speech toward our faith. But perhaps in our rush to defend ourselves, we are missing the larger truth that Ventura and Turner have unconsciously stumbled upon. Yes, it is true. Jesus is for the weak. Jesus is for the poor. Jesus is for "losers." Jesus is for those who come to the end of themselves and look to God for deliverance. "Weak" is a four-letter word for self-sufficient, boastful entrepreneurs. But Christians see that the world's understanding of strength is backwards—that true strength is made most visible in intentional weakness.

The apostle Paul wrote about a "thorn in the flesh"—an unnamed weakness that kept him from being satisfied in his ministry. Paul pleaded with the Lord to remove the thorn, but Jesus responded: "My grace is sufficient for you, for my power is made perfect in weakness." Paul discovered that God's perspective differed greatly from the world's view of power. "For the sake of Christ, then, I am content with weaknesses. . . . For when I am weak, then I am strong."[10]

Caesar and Jesus

Consider Jesus of Nazareth alongside Caesar Augustus. At the time of Christ's birth, Caesar had issued a call to the Roman world that everyone be counted and properly taxed. As he enjoyed luxurious accommodations in his Roman palace, he hoped to demonstrate his own greatness before a watching world by publicizing the great number of people under his domain. And yet in an unnoticed corner of Caesar's kingdom, in a simple stable, sleeping in a feeding trough, the Son of God had come to show the glory of his Father.

The nature of infancy teaches us something about weakness, and it teaches us something about our God. Every Christmas, we celebrate not Caesar's triumphant census, but our Emmanuel. "God with us." The apostle Paul tells us that Jesus made himself a servant. The infinite God enclosed himself in a woman's womb for nine months. God the Son was wrapped in swaddling clothes and placed in a manger for a bed. God made himself vulnerable.

Picture Jesus, the firstborn above all creation, the One through whom God spoke the creation of the universe, sitting on his mother Mary's lap, learning to read and write! Such mysteries can never be fully explained. But it is the story of God's coming to earth—God's being with us—that lies at the heart of the Christian worldview.

Imagine Caesar in his palace and Jesus in the manger. Which one looks more like a king? What would you do if you were in Bethlehem at the time and you had to choose to pledge your allegiance to either a baby boy who excited a few rugged shepherds, or the ruler of the known world with an army of thousands at his command? Who was more powerful? Jesus or Caesar? Things are not always as they appear.

Christians must have a radically different conception of power. After all, when Jesus was crucified, it appeared that he was dying as a weak man at the hands of the strong. Pilate appeared to have the authority and power. "We have no king but Caesar!" the people shouted. Caesar ruled by conquering lands and subjugating people. Jesus conquered sin, death, and the grave by suffering and dying—by bearing the full weight of God's wrath toward the evil of the world and then rising again to new life.

The Great Reversal

The cross is the climax of the great themes of reversal found throughout the Old and New Testaments. In Mary's song, often called the "Magnificat," she speaks of the mighty being brought down from their thrones and God's exaltation of the humble. She sings about the rich being sent away empty and the hungry being filled with good things. In the kingdom of God, everything is being turned upside down.[11]

God's view of our world is radically different from our own. History books about ancient Egypt list all the Pharaohs and their accomplishments. It is interesting to note that the Bible never tells us the name of Pharaoh during Moses' day. However, in the book of Exodus, we are given the names of the two Hebrew midwives who protected the Israelite babies, defying Pharaoh's orders.[12] From God's point of view, the faithfulness of Shiphrah and Puah are far more important than the pyramids of Rameses the Great.

And nowhere is the "Great Reversal" more evident than in the seeming weakness of the Lamb who is slain and yet sitting on the throne in Revelation. The slain lamb would appear to be a picture of ultimate weakness, and yet a glimpse of God's throne room shows us that Jesus is the conquering King who has won the victory through his death and resurrection.[13]

Power in the biblical sense affirms God's glory, not our own. We should take the earthly power and authority that God has given us and exercise it in such a way that it shines a spotlight on God's magnificent grace.

In order to subvert the Caesar of Power, we must be ready to question the world's derision of apparent weakness. It is often in our weaknesses that God's strength is most clearly perceived, and it is often in doing something the world sees as backwards that we are taking spiritual steps forward.

The Puritan prayer captures this truth well:

Let me learn by paradox that the way down is the way up,
that to be low is to be high,
that the broken heart is the healed heart,
that the contrite spirit is the rejoicing spirit,
that the repenting soul is the victorious soul,
that to have nothing is to possess all,
that to give is to receive,
that the valley is the place of vision.[14]

Learning to Share Power

Subversive churches share power. Congregations that share power ensure that authority is spread out among many wise believers.

Different denominations have different church polities. Some churches are run by the pastor and a deacon board. Others have a plurality of ruling elders. Some churches are instructed by a denominational hierarchy outside the local congregation. Others are run by various committees.

There are strengths and weaknesses in each model of church government, and this is not the place to debate which model represents the biblical picture most faithfully. Regardless of the polity of the local congregation, church members can avoid concentrating all power in one place by voluntarily sharing power among themselves.

Learning from Each Other

Sharing power means that even those in positions of authority recognize that they are part of a learning community. A few years ago, I heard a mega-church pastor speaking about the importance of listening for God's voice in the church. He mentioned that he had been given an audio sermon preached by a seminary student on a well-known passage of Scripture. The pastor told the congregation that he not only listened to the student's preaching, but that he had gained some valuable insights into the biblical text that he had never considered before. There, before a watching world, a mega-church pastor at the pinnacle of "ministry success" was telling his congregation that he could learn from a beginning seminary student! Whenever we joyfully seek to learn from others, even those who we may think have less to offer, we are subverting the Caesar of Power.

There is a mentally handicapped man at my church named Larry. Larry never misses a service. He comes forward every Sunday to ask for prayer. He often speaks up in the prayer meeting or during Sunday school. Larry can't read or write, but he listens attentively to the teaching (and usually asks someone else to take notes for him). Always burdened for others, Larry never fails to have a prayer request. And he demonstrates a faithfulness to church attendance that exceeds that of many other church members. One Sunday morning, he thought he had missed his ride, and so he walked several miles to get to church!

I have come to appreciate Larry. Sometimes, his childlike comments are incisive. Whereas the world might look at a man like Larry and think he has nothing to contribute, the church should keep its ears open—ready to be challenged by "the least of these" among us.

Openness and Honesty

Of course, sharing power does not mean that authoritative leadership is unimportant. God has given pastors authority in the local church, and to deny a pastor this authority is to go against the biblical intention. Leadership can be abused. But the abuse of power does not mean that power should not exist. Churches must intentionally work to form structures that share power— not allowing one group or person to dominate the direction of the church.

One way that churches can subvert the Caesar of Power is by having business meetings that are open to the public. Certainly some matters should be confidential. Biblical wisdom and caution should inform which matters are best left unspoken. But adopting an attitude of openness and transparency before the congregation and the wider community provides a compelling testimony to outsiders. Whereas businesses may shred confidential documents, reports, and statistics in fear that they may fall into the wrong hands, churches should exhibit an openness to evaluation and critique that can serve as an added incentive for financial accountability.

Sharing power also takes place as the congregation looks to bring new people into leadership positions. When one group dominates the discussion for too long, devotion to the Caesar of Power can become a temptation. Churches must consistently eschew the trappings of power, and one way we do that is by discipling new people and raising up new leaders.

Limiting Our Power

Often we can subvert the Caesar of Power by refusing to exert lawful influence or authority. There may be times, for example, when a pastor has the rightful authority to hire a certain staff member, but refrains because of the hesitation of many godly people in the church. Being entrusted with authority does not necessarily mean that we must exert authority in every circumstance.

By placing limitations around our power, we are following after Jesus, who limited his power for God's glory. When he was tempted in the wilderness, Jesus had every right to turn stones into bread and to use his power for his own benefit.[15] But behind this seemingly innocuous action was the choice regarding what kind of Messiah Jesus would be: self-*serving* or self-*sacrificing*.

Later, the Gospel of John tells us that Jesus' audience was clamoring for a sign. Jesus could have done something miraculous to receive their allegiance. However, he refrained from exercising his power because he understood the wrongheaded notions of discipleship present in his listeners.[16] Christians who have been placed in positions of authority must be ever aware of the seemingly innocent exertions of authority that may indeed be driven by a more subtle, insidious desire for control.

Using Power as a Way to Serve Others

When his disciples argued over who would be the greatest in the kingdom, Jesus described the qualities that accompany God-defined greatness. He pushed the disciples beyond the seeking of man-centered earthly positions by holding up his own life as the example of ultimate greatness: the one who suffered, who served others, and who sacrificed his own life as the ransom for many.[17]

Jesus' different way of exercising his kingship probably puzzled the disciples. He had not come to be served and pampered as the kings of this world. His purpose would be fulfilled in serving others and sacrificing his own life so that others would be able to live eternally. Jesus affirmed that, in God's eyes, the greatest people are those who roll up their sleeves and get down to the dirty work of helping others, no matter how difficult the task may be.

Although the apostle John was one of the disciples who hoped that day to find a position of honor in the coming kingdom, he later understood the lesson Jesus was trying to get across to his followers. Later, John would write, "By this we know love, that he laid down his life for us, and we ought to lay down our lives for the brothers."[18] John eventually came to understand that greatness meant going the way of love, even when that meant walking the path to the cross.

We live in a day where everyone wants to be number one. Everyone is trying to be first in line, king of the hill, successful at the expense of everyone else. Jesus redefined greatness by stretching out his hands, denying himself, and taking up his cross. Jesus is the ultimate example of what greatness is in the eyes of God.

In God's eyes, it does not matter how much you acquire in the eyes of others, or how popular you are, or how successful your business is, or how much earthly authority you have. True greatness means suffering, service, and sacrifice. Whereas the world may estimate our rank and authority by how many people are serving us, God estimates our rank by how many people we are serving.

Power must be redefined as servanthood. Bernard of

HOLY SUBVERSION

Clairvaux once said, "If you are to do the work of a prophet, what you need is not a scepter but a hoe." In other words, get busy with the little, seemingly insignificant tasks that benefit others and not yourself. If you are too big for a little place, you are too little for a big place.

We subvert the Caesar of Power whenever we exert authority on behalf of others and not ourselves. In the book of Acts, Luke describes a situation in which Paul and Barnabas perform some miraculous signs and then discover that the townspeople are ready to worship them. How tempting it might have been for Paul and Barnabas to ride the wave of popularity and enjoy the worship of adoring fans. But Paul and Barnabas stopped the people at once.[19] Their good works had been on behalf of others in order to show the glory of God, not for themselves in order to bring honor to their own name.

Authority and power are not bad in and of themselves. The world sees them as means to an end, generally a very selfish end. Christians must see authority and power as gifts from God to be used *for others*.

HUMBLE AUTHORITY

A story is told about Francis of Assisi out in the woods one afternoon, seeking his friend, Bernard. Francis called out to him several times but to no avail. In his frustration, Francis decided he should go pray. The Holy Spirit revealed to Francis that Bernard had not heard him because he had been experiencing a particularly profound time of prayer. Francis was instantly ashamed of his anger. When he met Bernard again, he asked him to punish his selfishness by walking on his face. Imagine being told to walk on the face of Francis of Assisi!

In a world in which people jockey for positions and walk over anyone who might get in their way so they can obtain power and prestige, we need more Christians who will follow the example of Christ. We should humble ourselves and shun worldly prestige by giving away power and authority. We should turn the world's idea of weakness on its head and demonstrate how the power of God is made manifest in what the world dismisses as worthless. We should place our sinful cravings for power at the feet of the cross, and then walk away from Golgotha with a renewed understanding of how our power can be redirected into service and sacrifice.

Jesus said it best: "Whoever exalts himself will be humbled, and whoever humbles himself will be exalted."[20]

SUBVERSIVE EVANGELISM
Subverting Caesar by Sharing Christ

HOW DOES OUR UNDERSTANDING OF the subversive nature
of Christian discipleship transform our evangelism? We live in
a time when proselytizing is considered *anathema* in the United
States. Many Caesars in our day seek to dominate the minds
and hearts of people around us, but perhaps the most insidious
of them all is Tolerance. This Caesar would have us adopt a plu-
ralistic mind-set that sees all religions as equally valid. Whenever we put the world's view of tolerance on the throne, we
either change the message (to make it less offensive) or we give
up evangelism completely.

Another aspect of American society that has influenced the
way we share the gospel is consumerism. Some evangelistic pleas
speak of Jesus as a product to be "tried out" and "tested." Can
you imagine the apostles telling people to give Jesus "a trial
run?" When we evangelize this way, we are unintentionally col-
luding with our culture in ways we may not see. I cannot help
but wonder if some evangelists fit the description of "peddlers"
of God's Word that the apostle Paul warned us about.[1]

If we are to reclaim evangelistic practices that are subversive of our culture's capitulation to tolerance or consumerism,
then we must be honest about the costs of following Christ,
declare Jesus as Lord over all of life, and proclaim him as the
only Savior.

SUBVERSIVE EVANGELISM PROCLAIMS THE COSTS OF THE CHRISTIAN LIFE

During my mission work in Romania, I discovered that the Romanian language did not have equivalent words for much of the evangelical lingo I was accustomed to using in the United States. For example, in one sermon, I wanted to urge people to "commit their lives to Christ." To my surprise, the Baptists in Romania frowned on such talk. One friend said, "Using the word 'commit' sounds like you are urging people to join a social club. We don't use the word 'commitment' for salvation."

"Well, what word *do* you use?" I asked.

"Surrender."

My Romanian friends, just coming out of Communist oppression in which repentance would entail persecution, saw evangelism as proclaiming God's call for people to enter into a new realm, a new way of seeing the world because of what Christ had done in history. Both Americans and Romanians emphasized repentance and faith, but I noticed the Romanians placed more emphasis on surrendering to the pursuit of a loving and sovereign King.

An Invitation with a Warning

When Jesus called people to himself, he seemed to vacillate between speaking of the benefits of salvation and the hardships that await believers. There is no question he spoke of salvation's rewards. Take a look at some of Jesus' words regarding the benefits of trusting in him:

> "Come to me, all who labor and are heavy laden, and I will give you rest. Take my yoke upon you, and learn from me, for I am gentle and lowly in heart, and you will find rest for your souls. For my yoke is easy, and my burden is light." (Matt. 11:28–30)

"If anyone thirsts, let him come to me and drink." (John 7:37)

"Truly, truly, I say to you, if anyone keeps my word, he will never see death." (John 8:51)

"I am the door. If anyone enters by me, he will be saved and will go in and out and find pasture. . . . I came that they may have life and have it abundantly. I am the good shepherd. The good shepherd lays down his life for the sheep." (John 10:9–11)

But Jesus also boldly told people to count the cost before following him. He warned them of the costs of discipleship and did not shy away from some "hard" sayings:

"If anyone comes to me and does not hate his own father and mother and wife and children and brothers and sisters, yes, and even his own life, he cannot be my disciple. Whoever does not bear his own cross and come after me cannot be my disciple. For which of you, desiring to build a tower, does not first sit down and count the cost, whether he has enough to complete it? . . . Or what king, going out to encounter another king in war, will not sit down first and deliberate whether he is able with ten thousand to meet him who comes against him with twenty thousand? . . . So therefore, any one of you who does not renounce all that he has cannot be my disciple." (Luke 14:26–28, 31, 33)

"Truly, truly, I say to you, unless you eat the flesh of the Son of Man and drink his blood, you have no life in you." (John 6:53)

"No one who puts his hand to the plow and looks back is fit for the kingdom of God." (Luke 9:62)

"How difficult it is for those who have wealth to enter the kingdom of God!" (Luke 18:24)

"The gate is narrow and the way is hard that leads to life, and those who find it are few." (Matt. 7:14)

With one hand, Jesus seemed to be calling people to himself, yet with the other hand, he seemed to be pushing people away. Salesmen focus on the benefits of purchasing a product; only after emphasizing the positives do they show people the fine print. Jesus did not engage in such tactics. He was honest about both the rewards of salvation and the costs of discipleship.

Too often, our evangelism centers primarily on the benefits of following Christ without a clear articulation of the costs. *Come to Christ so you can go to heaven! Come to Christ and he will prosper your finances! Come to Christ and your life will be so much easier!* Only after people make decisions are they told they need to go to church, start reading their Bibles, stop living with their boyfriend, etc.

But coming to Christ does not promise us a comfortable life. Dietrich Bonhoeffer, in *The Cost of Discipleship*, wrote:

> When Christ calls a man, he bids him come and die. It may be a death like that of the first disciples who had to leave home and work to follow him, or it may be a death like Luther's, who had to leave the monastery and go out into the world. But it is the same death every time—death in Jesus Christ, the death of the old man at his call.[2]

Coming to Christ actually complicates our lives. We no longer make decisions based on our selfish preferences. We weigh options, take into consideration their spiritual effects, and seek to align ourselves with the revealed will of God.

The way of Jesus is often one of intense suffering. It is no wonder that many people who make professions of faith in our churches quickly disappear. The easy life they were promised never comes. Like seeds in shallow soil, they spring up for a time and then wither away under the heat of the sun.[3]

To seek a life of Christian ease and comfort is to seek a false

Christ. We do not call people to Christ because Christianity is easy. We call people to Christ because Christianity is true. And evangelism that subverts the Caesar of Consumerism will speak truthfully regarding the costs of discipleship.

SUBVERSIVE EVANGELISM PROCLAIMS THAT JESUS IS LORD OVER ALL OF LIFE

One of the reasons the Roman emperors saw Christianity as a threat to the empire was that the Christian confession that "Jesus is Lord" affected every area of the believers' lives. Belief in the resurrection of Jesus transformed one's view of reality. Whereas the upper class of Roman society would have seen the kingdom of Caesar Augustus as the bright light of human history and the extension of Roman power as the inevitable triumph of progress, Christians viewed history as reaching its climax one weekend in Jerusalem, when a crucified Messiah came back from the dead.

"Jesus Christ is the true Lord of the world and he will return to judge the living and the dead." Such a message necessarily affected all of reality and countered the Roman idea of triumph and progress.

The Religious Drawer

It is common for many Christians in the West today to see their religious faith as just one aspect of their lives. Picture your life as a chest of drawers. You have a drawer for work. You have a drawer for entertainment. You have another for family. And over to the side is a drawer that contains your religious practices.

Many Christians open up the religious drawer on Sundays and go through the motions of attending church, reciting the creeds, singing, and praying. But on Sunday afternoon, they shut the drawer until the next weekend. The religious drawer does not impinge upon the other drawers at all. It stays nicely tucked away in a corner, off to the side. Entertainment choices, leisure time, our ideas of success, our work ethic, the way we spend our money, our sexual choices—each of these other drawers is left untouched. We may affirm that Jesus is Lord of all, but our lives show that Jesus is Lord only of our religious practices.

But think about this: if our faith is only applicable to "sacred practices" (like Bible study, prayer, and church attendance), then we have a faith that has little to say about what we do with the vast majority of our time. Christianity becomes a mere addition to an old way of life.

The biblical picture is much richer. And it is this biblical picture that we are called to proclaim to those around us. "Jesus is Lord" is an announcement that applies to every aspect of our lives. It is not subversive at all to worship Jesus in the privacy of our religious lives. The church is counter-cultural by proclaiming Jesus as Lord over every area of life, not just our religious activities.

We cannot divide up our lives into "sacred" aspects and "secular" aspects, as if Jesus were Lord of only our sacred practices. The Bible teaches that every area of the Christian's life should be sacred—set apart under the lordship of Christ. Our labor must be unto the Lord just as our leisure must be unto the Lord.[4] We do not confess that Jesus is Lord of only one drawer in the chest. He is the chest's Maker, and he becomes the chest's Redeemer—having purchased *all the drawers* with his precious blood.

The Gospel as Public News

Christians practice subversive evangelism by proclaiming the public nature of the gospel message. The early Christians were not merely spreading some helpful advice about spirituality. They were announcing the good news that Jesus of Nazareth had died for their sins and had been raised to new life three days later. This news brought with it a complete reordering not only of one's religious beliefs, but also of one's view of society, work, government, and money.

We do not share the gospel as a bit of religious advice to help people feel better with whatever idolatries they have. We preach a gospel that is public news, a message about a risen Christ who, in giving his life to purchase our salvation, has demolished all idols.

SUBVERSIVE EVANGELISM PROCLAIMS JESUS AS THE ONLY SAVIOR

Our affirmation that Jesus Christ is Lord not only refers to his being Lord over every area of our lives, but also refers to his being the only Savior. The claim of exclusivity is highly unpopular in our day, even among some evangelicals. But compromise on this issue leads us to collude with the Caesar of Tolerance.

Whenever Larry King interviews pastors on *Larry King Live,* he inevitably asks them if they believe Jesus is the only way to God. Larry has always had a knack for peeling back the layers of an issue and piercing right to the heart of a controversy. Regarding the exclusivity of faith in Jesus Christ for salvation, Larry senses a tender spot in the theology of many evangelicals. After all, as a Jew, Larry knows that if the pastor affirms Jesus' exclusivity, the pastor is implying that Larry is under divine condemnation. That is why most pastors capitulate under the pressure. And so the answers begin to get mushy:

"Only God truly knows the heart."

"Who's to say? I just don't know."

"Jesus is the only *guaranteed* way to heaven."

"I'll leave that up to God."

Our Way or The Way?

Affirming Jesus Christ as the only way of salvation seems especially arrogant and intolerant in this postmodern age. But Jesus himself has left us little choice in the matter. He claims to be the Way, the Truth, and the Life, and he says no one comes to God the Father except through him.[5]

I have heard one pastor try to create a mediating position by affirming that "Jesus is *our* only way to God." But if we add the word "our," we are implying something akin to our society's faulty view of truth. We are communicating to the world: "This is *our* truth, but it might not be everyone's truth."

Jesus does not qualify his exclusiveness and uniqueness. He adds no additional words. Notice that he does not say to his disciples, "I'm *your* way to God. *None of you* can get to God except through me." No. Jesus purposefully claims divinity and uniqueness for himself and leaves that statement unqualified. The testimony of the early church was the same. The apostle Peter famously preached that "there is no other name" by which people can be saved.[6]

This doctrine has long been counter-cultural. The early Christians were thrown to the lions and burnt alive in royal gardens—not because they were saying that Jesus was *a* way to God, but because they were claiming that he was *the* way. By proclaiming Jesus as *the* Lord, they were pledging allegiance to someone greater than Caesar. That was the belief that unmasked Rome's hypocritical "tolerance" and unleashed waves of severe persecution.

The great Caesar of our time is a religious pluralism that relegates all religious claims to mere private opinions. The pluralism of our day demands that all religions give up their claims to truth in favor of an illogical idea that all religions can basically be good, true, and equally valid in their own way. The pluralist philosophy sweeping through the West today has no problem with individuals seeking to better their private spiritual lives. One only gets castigated for making a truth claim said to be true for everyone.

It takes no courage at all for a Christian to proclaim that "Jesus is *our* way to God" (with the implication that other people have other ways to God). A truly courageous Christian will stand against the tide of relativism and affirm the witness of the New Testament by saying, "Jesus is the *only* way to God."

Exposing the Myth of Tolerance

When we affirm this watershed doctrine, we quickly discover that our culture's myth of tolerance is exposed. In the name of tolerance, we find that such religious exclusiveness cannot be tolerated. It is sadly ironic that we who conscientiously seek to safeguard a truth that has been proclaimed by the church for two thousand years would be seen as arrogant and bigoted, while a society that would have us renounce our beliefs at the altar of religious pluralism would be seen as "tolerant" and "broadminded."

I have found that people of other religions are rarely offended by the idea that Jesus is the only way to God. Muslims who believe that Islam is the one true faith are not surprised, and indeed, expect me as a Christian to argue forcefully for the uniqueness of Jesus. Generally, those who are most offended are the nominally religious (or agnostic) people who believe the myth that all religions are basically the same and that exclusivity is intolerant.

Respecting People in Other Faiths

Proclaiming the exclusivity of Christianity's truth claims is the first step toward respecting people of other faiths. Whenever someone tells me that all religions are basically the same, I usually ask them to show more respect to the adherents of other religions. Even a cursory study will show major differences in the religions' beliefs about God, humanity, salvation, and eternity. We should have enough respect for people of other faiths to charitably disagree and not patronize them with silly declarations that "our different beliefs are really the same deep down."

When someone accuses me of intolerance for believing that only one religion can be true, I point to the fact that the vast majority of people in the world today believe their religion is the right religion and that all others are wrong. To me, it is more arrogant to assume that finally, we in the enlightened West have discovered that no religion is true and that all the religious people in the world are deluded, still living in the Dark Ages.[7]

Proclaiming the exclusivity of Jesus Christ for salvation does not have to be a demeaning doctrine, a truth used to berate people for not trusting in Christ. Jesus tells us to love our enemies, and he demonstrated his love for rebellious humanity by sacrificing his life for our salvation. We are not seeking to impose Christianity upon anyone else, but only to make a case for its truth claims. If anything, it is pluralism that seeks to impose itself, by forcing its relativism upon all religions.

MAKING DISCIPLES OF ALL NATIONS

Subversive evangelism takes place whenever someone shares the gospel message faithfully and refuses to shy away from its harder truths. Unfortunately, we rarely talk today about converting people to Christianity. In fact, many Christians (especially in the "Bible Belt") rarely speak of unsaved people as "lost." Instead, we speak of "the unchurched." For many, the goal of evangelism is for people to become "churched." We hope to reach nominal Christians and make them active Christians.

This kind of "evangelism" is not true evangelism at all.

It may do some good in the short term, but it is certainly not subversive of the Caesar of Tolerance. Christians should not be ashamed to make concerted efforts to reach Jews, Muslims, Hindus, and Buddhists for Jesus Christ. We have been commissioned to boldly proclaim the gospel and to call people to salvation. The apostle Paul would not have seen such evangelism as prejudiced against people of other faiths. More likely, he would have seen our neglect of people of other races and religions as prejudice. It is precisely because we believe that Jesus is the only Savior that we can proclaim the gospel to all creation.

Called to Love, Not Tolerance

Many today seem to define tolerance as never disagreeing with anyone about any religious matter. But does not the very notion of tolerance assume some sort of disagreement? To seek to win someone over to another viewpoint is not intolerance. Debate takes place in universities, churches, and businesses all the time.

But even this kind of tolerance is not our goal. We are not merely called to tolerate those who disagree with us; we are called to love. The world's idea of tolerance is a parody of the Christian understanding of love.

Tolerance is passive. Love is active.

Tolerance is a feeling of apathy. Love is accompanied by feelings of great affection.

Tolerance keeps people at arm's length in hopes of not offending them. Love embraces people where they are and "hopes all things."

Tolerance leaves people alone as individuals. Love ushers people into a community of generosity.

Tolerance keeps a safe distance between those in need. Love rolls up its sleeves in service even to those who may be unlikable.

Tolerance avoids confrontation in order to maintain "peace." Love tells the truth boldly and graciously in order to bring about a deeper, more lasting peace.

If ever there was a disciple that Jesus could have "tolerated," it would have been Judas Iscariot. But the apostle John tells us that Jesus "loved his disciples fully" right before Jesus rolled up his sleeves and started washing their feet, even the feet of the one who would betray him! You don't have to look further than Jesus to see how his teaching about loving one's enemies finds its true expression. The love Jesus had for us did not just warm his heart; it led him to a Roman cross.[8]

Our evangelistic efforts should not be about building big churches in order to increase our glory before a watching world. We share the gospel with friends and neighbors because doing so honors the Savior who gave his life for us. By unashamedly participating in evangelism, we are striking down the Caesar of Tolerance and putting the love of Jesus Christ on the throne—a hard and costly love that demonstrates itself in our efforts to bring others to faith.

THE SUBVERSIVE COMMUNITY

I am convinced that one reason why it is difficult for many people to see anything greater than the ultimate goal of "tolerance" in our day is that they have never experienced the genuine love of a Christian community. By putting on display a different way of life, we are telling the world there is another way to live and there is a love that is greater than mere tolerance.

We cannot live our faith alone. We can do many of the things mentioned in this book as individuals, but it is the presence of such a radical lifestyle within a community that makes the greatest impact. An allegiance to Christ the King that is truly subversive must be displayed within the context of a community of faith.

I used to believe that Christians who thought of evangelism as inviting people to church were taking the easy way out. (I still think church members should be equipped to share the gospel in a one-on-one setting.) But there is indeed something profound in inviting lost people to see the Christian community. Very few people will trust Christ because of intellectual reasoning or apologetic proofs. Most people will come to faith only after seeing the church doing what she has been called to do: living under the lordship of Jesus Christ.

What better way to proclaim that Jesus is Lord than to invite people into a community of faith in which Jesus' lordship is on display? This is where discipleship and evangelism meet.

As we grow in our discipleship, and as our allegiance to Jesus becomes more and more subversive of the world around us, our lives begin to better reflect our King. When our message that "there is another king" is backed up by a community in loving submission to that King, the power of God unto salvation is made manifest. People fall upon the mercy of God for salvation and find themselves birthed into the kingdom of light.

AFTERWORD

IN THE FIRST CHAPTER OF THIS BOOK, I mentioned that the first-century Roman emperor Domitian signed his documents as "God"—a blasphemous practice intended to reaffirm his own exalted understanding of himself. Domitian was expressing publicly his attempt to live as his own god and king. Though we may shake our heads in amazement at the obsessive egotism that would lead a king to so openly challenge the authority of God, we also are often guilty of living as if we were God. We live as if we too were signing all our decisions: "God."

The main thrust of this book has been a call to reclaiming the subversive nature of Christian discipleship. Christians confess that Jesus is Lord and strive to live in accordance with that confession. We have seen that discipleship encompasses all of life, and that our allegiance to Christ the King should subvert "Caesars" like Money, Sex, and Power.

I have chosen to describe only a handful of rivals to Christ's lordship. Certainly, there are others we could have mentioned: fashion, food, family, ministry, etc. There is no limit to the idolatries the human heart can manufacture. We must, as churches, think through ways that we can undermine these idols before a watching world. Our goal must be to identify the prevailing idolatries of our culture and then to deliberately subvert them.

Christians have been delivered from slavery to our own selfish desires and whims. We have been bought with a price. God has redeemed us with the precious blood of his Son. And now, Christians are called to proclaim the truthfulness of Christianity.

We have been commissioned as ambassadors of King Jesus—sent out into the world with the announcement of what Jesus' life, death, and resurrection have accomplished.

In previous generations, when Christians proclaimed that Jesus of Nazareth, crucified for our sins and raised for our justification, is the true Lord of the world, skeptics tended to respond by saying, "Prove it." A defense of the reasonableness of Christianity guaranteed a hearing for the gospel.

Today, when we proclaim that Jesus is Lord, disillusioned skeptics tend to respond by saying, "Show me." A community living according to the gospel helps provide space for people to consider the truth claims of Christianity.

When we confess with our mouths that Jesus is Lord, we should demonstrate with our lives the truth of that confession. Our task is to live in such a way that the world sees our decisions and choices as being influenced by Jesus Christ—our great God and King. Serving Christ subverts Caesar.

My hope is that Christians will not merely be prepared to answer the people who ask us about the hope that is within us. I pray that, first and foremost, our lives of holy subversion will be what causes people to begin asking questions in the first place.

ACKNOWLEDGMENTS

THERE IS NO WAY TO ACKNOWLEDGE all of the people who have influenced the writing in this book. We are shaped by our experiences and formed by the people who have discipled us and taught us the truths of the Christian faith. I am grateful for a Christian heritage in my family that goes back several generations. My grandparents and parents have instilled in me a profound trust in the authority of God's Word and the transformative power of the gospel.

I am greatly indebted to friends who offered gentle criticism and terrific insight: Phillip Bethancourt, Eric Peterson, Robbie Sagers, Terry Delaney, Tony Kummer, Darryl Dash, Nick Mitchell, and Kevin DeYoung. My brother Justin also gave me good feedback, as did my father. My pastor, Kevin Minchey, has been unflagging in his support of this project. Members of my church family provided helpful advice as well: Alan and Sheila Lovelace, Scott Long, and Tyler Miller. Several biblical scholars have given me insight into early Christianity. Gregg Allison, Michael Haykin, Radu Gheorghita, and Russell Moore.

It has been a joy to work with the team at Crossway and to benefit from the wisdom of Justin Taylor, James Kinnard, Sherah Grose, and the other editors.

I am honored by the endorsements of the pastors, scholars, and authors who took the time to read and recommend this work.

Most of all, I am grateful to my wife, Corina, for helping me carve out the time necessary for this project. She has always supported my writing efforts, and her constant love and encouragement sustained me during the process of writing this book.

NOTES

Foreword

1. See "Americans Are Most Likely to Base Truth on Feelings," The Barna Group, February 12, 2002, http://www.barna.org/barna-update/article/5-barna-update/67-americans-are-most-likely-to-base-truth-on-feelings.com.

2. Brad J. Waggoner, *The Shape of Faith to Come* (Nashville: B&H Publishing Group, 2008).

Chapter 1: Jesus and the Gospel of Caesar

1. For an example of the exalted language given to the Roman emperors, see Wilhelm Dittenberger, ed., *Orientis graeci inscriptions selectee*, vol. 2, #458 (Leipzig, 1903–1905). Also, Ethelbert Stauffer, *Christ and the Caesars* (Eugene, OR: Wipf & Stock Publishers, 2008) lists many parallels between Christian proclamation and the cult of Caesar-worship. A more recent book by Seyoon Kim, *Christ and Caesar: The Gospel and the Roman Empire in the Writings of Paul and Luke* (Grand Rapids, MI: Wm. B. Eerdmans, 2008) demonstrates how the early Christians' use of imperial rhetoric was not an attempt to bring about a political revolution, but a way of highlighting the inherent difference between the kingdoms of this world and the kingdom of Christ.

2. For this and other accounts of the Caesars' desire for titles of divinity, see the ancient historian Suetonius, *The Lives of the Twelve Caesars—Complete* (Teddington, Middlesex: Echo Library, 2006).

3. Luke 13:1–5 records an example of Pontius Pilate slaughtering pious Jews at the altar, so that the blood of these Jews mixed with the blood from their animal sacrifices.

4. See Rom. 10:9.

5. See Acts 4:12.

6. See Matt. 28:18.

7. See Phil. 2:10–11.

8. N. T. Wright, *The Challenge of Jesus: Rediscovering Who Jesus Was and Is* (Downers Grove, IL: Intervarsity Press, 1999), 131–32.

9. In Romans 13, the apostle Paul writes about the role and authority of earthly governors. Yet even here, he subverts the Roman system by placing the human Caesar under the rule and authority of God. Likewise, in a letter to Christians facing persecution, the apostle Peter urges people to submit to earthly authority and honor the emperor (1 Pet. 2:13–17).

10. Eph. 6:12.

11. Acts 2:36.

12. Matt. 6:24, NKJV.

Chapter 2: Subverting The Self

1. Rhonda Byrne, *The Secret* (New York: Atria Books, 2006), 183.

2. Ibid., 164.

3. Christian Smith with Melinda Lundquist Denton, *Soul Searching: The Religious and Spiritual Lives of American Teenagers* (Oxford University Press, 2005).

4. 1 Cor. 15:28.

5. Bill Bright, "Have You Heard of the Four Spiritual Laws?" copyright 1965 by Campus Crusade for Christ, New Life Publications.

6. See John 16:33.

7. The emphasis on waiting for your best life later comes from a chapel message by Russell D. Moore at The Southern Baptist Theological Seminary, February 1, 2007: "So Maybe Denial *Is* a River in Egypt: Blessing, Ministry, and Your Best Life Later."

8. "Article V: God's Purpose of Grace" in "The Baptist Faith and Message," http://www.sbc.net/bfm/bfm2000.asp#iv.

9. See 1 Pet. 1:12.

10. Rom. 5:8.

11. Eph. 1:10.

12. Eph. 1:21.

13. Bob Kauflin, "Let Your Kingdom Come," Sovereign Grace Praise, 2006.

14. Charles H. Spurgeon, "January 28," *Evening by Evening* (Wheaton, IL: Crossway, 2007), 36.

15. Eph. 2:4–5.

16. John Stott, *The Message of Galatians* (Downers Grove, IL: InterVarsity Press, 1984), 179.

17. Scot McKnight writes, "A local church *always* performs the gospel it proclaims." *Embracing Grace: A Gospel for All of Us* (Brewster, MA: Paraclete Press, 2005), 11.

18. Gen. 12:1–3.

19. Genesis 41–47.

20. Matt. 5:14–16.

21. Isa. 49:6; Acts 13:47

22. Eph. 4:1–6; Col. 1:18.

23. Eph. 5:22–33.

Chapter 3: Subverting Success

1. See John 15:2.

2. See John 6.

3. 1 Cor. 2:4–5.

4. Acts 2:47.

5. See Tertullian, *Apologeticus*, ch. 50, in Otto Bardenhewer, *Patrology: The Lives and Works of the Fathers of the Church*, trans. Thomas J. Shahan (Freiburg im Breisgau and St. Louis: B. Herder, 1908).

6. Rom. 8:18.

7. Eph. 4:3.

Chapter 4: Subverting Money

1. Heather Donahoe, "Storage Space Grows and Grows . . . " *The Tennessean,* May 12, 2008.

2. Matt. 6:24.

3. 1 Tim. 6:10.

4. Gen. 4:1–16.

5. Joshua 7.

6. Joseph Mallia and Matthew Chayes, "Wal-Mart Worker Dies in Black Friday Stampede," *Newsday,* November 28, 2008. http://www.newsday.com/news/local/nassau/ny-limart1129,0,167903.story.

7. James 2:1–13.

8. John Mayer, "Something's Missing," from the album *Heavier Things* (Sony Music, 2003).

9. Kenneth Bailey fills in some of the historical details of this parable in his book *Through Peasant Eyes* (Grand Rapids, MI: Wm. B. Eerdmans, 1980), 57–73.

10. Luke 19:1–10.

11. Col. 3:5.

12. Acts 20:35.

13. Eph. 4:28.

14. See Luke 12:48.

15. C.S. Lewis, *Mere Christianity* (New York: Macmillan Publishing Company, 1952), 82.

16. Matt. 6:19–21.

17. Office of News and Communications, Duke University, "Conservative Protestants' Religious Beliefs Contribute to Their Low Wealth, Duke Study Shows: Duke Sociology Professor Lisa A. Keister Examines How Religion Affects the Wealth of Believers" (www.dukenews.duke.edu/2008/03/cprelease.html, acccessed March 24, 2008).

18. Luke 21:1–4.

19. Geoff Moore and the Distance, "Only a Fool," from the album *Threads* (Forefront, 1997).

Chapter 5: Subverting Leisure

1. The contrasts between *1984* and *Brave New World* are laid out in the foreword to Neil Postman's *Amusing Ourselves to Death: Public Discourse in an Age of Show Business* (New York: Penguin Books, 1986).

2. Gen. 1:1–2:2.

3. See Gen. 2:3; Ex. 20:8–11.

4. Col. 3:17.

5. "What's ahead for Net, digital entertainment," USAToday.com, May 11, 2005, http://www.usatoday.com/tech/news/2005-05-11-roundtable-usat_x.htm.

6. John Piper, *Don't Waste Your Life* (Wheaton, IL: Crossway, 2003), 120.

7. Juvenal, *Satire* 10.77–81, late first century or early second century AD.

8. 1 Tim. 4:7–8.

9. 2 Tim. 2:5.

10. 2 Tim. 4:7.

11. Phil. 3:13–14.

12. See Tertullian's Letter "On Spectacles" or Cyprian's Epistle to Donatus.

13. Matt. 6:33.

14. John 20:21.

15. Mark 12:30.

16. "You (Are a Human Animal)" from *The Mickey Mouse Club*, found on *Disney Sing-Along Songs 2: The Bare Necessities*, VHS (Walt Disney Video, 1994).

17. James 4:14.

18. See Matt. 6:25–34.

19. Francis Schaeffer, *No Little People* (Wheaton, IL: Crossway, 2003), 86–87.

20. 1 Pet. 4:7.

Chapter 6: Subverting Sex

1. Gen. 1:28.
2. Gen. 2:18–25.
3. Lauren Winner, *Real Sex: The Naked Truth about Chastity* (Grand Rapids, MI: Brazos Press, 2005), 38.
4. C. S. Lewis, *Mere Christianity* (New York: Touchstone Books, 1996), 97.
5. Stanley M. Hauerwas and William H. Willimon, *The Truth about God: The Ten Commandments in Christian Life* (Nashville: Abingdon, 1999), 97.
6. See Eph. 5:22–33.
7. Ps. 127:3–5.
8. Gen. 9:1, 7.
9. Aron tells his story in more detail in *Between a Rock and a Hard Place* (New York: Atria Books, 2005).

Chapter 7: Subverting Power

1. Gen. 1:26–30.
2. Gen. 2:19–20.
3. Numbers 16.
4. Num. 20:10–13; Deut. 32:48–52.
5. See Romans 13.
6. 1 Tim. 2:1–4.
7. Gen. 3:5.
8. Saul's pursuit of David takes place in 1 Samuel 19–27.
9. Rom. 1:1; Phil. 1:1.
10. 2 Cor. 12:1–10.
11. Luke 1:46–55.
12. Ex. 1:8–22.
13. Rev. 5:6–13.
14. Prayer excerpt from Arthur Bennett, *The Valley of Vision: A Collection of Puritan Prayers and Devotions* (East Peoria: Banner of Truth Trust, 2005), introductory prayer.
15. See Matt. 4:1–11; Luke 4:1–13.
16. John 6:22–71.
17. Mark 10:32–45.
18. 1 John 3:16.
19. Acts 14:8–18.
20. Matt. 23:12.

Chapter 8: Subversive Evangelism

1. 2 Cor. 2:17.
2. Dietrich Bonhoeffer, *The Cost of Discipleship* (New York: Touchstone, 1959, 1995), 89–90.
3. Matt. 13:5–6, 20–21.
4. Col. 3:23–24.
5. John 14:6.
6. Acts 4:10–12.
7. Tim Keller makes this point well in *The Reason for God: Belief in an Age of Skepticism* (New York: Dutton, 2008), 11–13.
8. N. T. Wright contrasts forgiveness with tolerance in *Evil and the Justice of God* (Downers Grove, IL: Intervarsity Press, 2006), 151–52.

SCRIPTURE INDEX